TEEN CHALLENGES

FAMILY CONFLICTS AND CHANGES

by Christa C. Hogan

CONTENT CONSULTANT

Kathleen N. Bergman, PhD
Research Assistant Professor, Psychology
University of Notre Dame

Essential Library

An Imprint of Abdo Publishing | abdobooks.com

ABDOBOOKS.COM

Published by Abdo Publishing, a division of ABDO, PO Box 398166, Minneapolis, Minnesota 55439. Copyright © 2022 by Abdo Consulting Group, Inc. International copyrights reserved in all countries. No part of this book may be reproduced in any form without written permission from the publisher. Essential Library™ is a trademark and logo of Abdo Publishing.

Printed in the United States of America, North Mankato, Minnesota.
102021
012022

THIS BOOK CONTAINS RECYCLED MATERIALS

Cover Photos: G-Stock Studio/iStockphoto, foreground; Africa Studio/Shutterstock Images, background
Interior Photos: Ryan J. Lane/iStockphoto, 4; Ronnachai Park/Shutterstock Images, 8; Motortion Films/Shutterstock Images, 12; Iakov Filimonov/Shutterstock Images, 14, 92; Rick Bowmer/AP Images, 18–19; Rawpixel/iStockphoto, 21, 44; Yakobchuk Viacheslav/Shutterstock Images, 26–27; Shutterstock Images, 28, 36, 43, 51, 60, 98–99; Monkey Business Images/iStockphoto, 33; iStockphoto, 38, 90; Pitiya Phinjongsakundit/Shutterstock Images, 48; Pixel-Shot/Shutterstock Images, 54–55; DGL Images/Shutterstock Images, 58–59; Baza Production/Shutterstock Images, 65; Syda Productions/Shutterstock Images, 68; Ann Gaysorn/Shutterstock Images, 70; G-Stock Studio/Shutterstock Images, 73; Antonio Diaz/Shutterstock Images, 77; Kosim Shukurov/Shutterstock Images, 80–81; Andriy Shevchuk/Shutterstock Images, 82; Alex Potemkin/iStockphoto, 88; Beatriz Vera/Shutterstock Images, 96

Editor: Megan Ellis
Series Designer: Colleen McLaren

LIBRARY OF CONGRESS CONTROL NUMBER: 2021941226

PUBLISHER'S CATALOGING-IN-PUBLICATION DATA

Names: Hogan, Christa C., author.

Title: Family conflicts and changes / by Christa C. Hogan

Description: Minneapolis, Minnesota : Abdo Publishing, 2022 | Series: Teen challenges | Includes online resources and index.

Identifiers: ISBN 9781532196270 (lib. bdg.) | ISBN 9781098218089 (ebook)

Subjects: LCSH: Families--Juvenile literature. | Family relationships--Juvenile literature. | Family problems--Juvenile literature. | Communication in families--Juvenile literature. | Family crises--Juvenile literature.

Classification: DDC 646.7--dc23

CONTENTS

CHAPTER ONE
FAMILIES, CONFLICT, AND CHANGE 04

CHAPTER TWO
COMMON FAMILY CHANGES 14

CHAPTER THREE
FAMILY DYNAMICS 28

CHAPTER FOUR
ADOLESCENCE AND FAMILY CONFLICT 38

CHAPTER FIVE
TYPES OF FAMILY CONFLICT 48

CHAPTER SIX
CONFLICT AND TRAUMA . . 60

CHAPTER SEVEN
COPING STRATEGIES AND SELF-CARE 70

CHAPTER EIGHT
HEALTHY CONFLICT RESOLUTION 82

CHAPTER NINE
LOOKING AHEAD 92

ESSENTIAL FACTS 100
GLOSSARY 102
ADDITIONAL RESOURCES 104
SOURCE NOTES 106
INDEX 110
ABOUT THE AUTHOR 112
ABOUT THE CONSULTANT 112

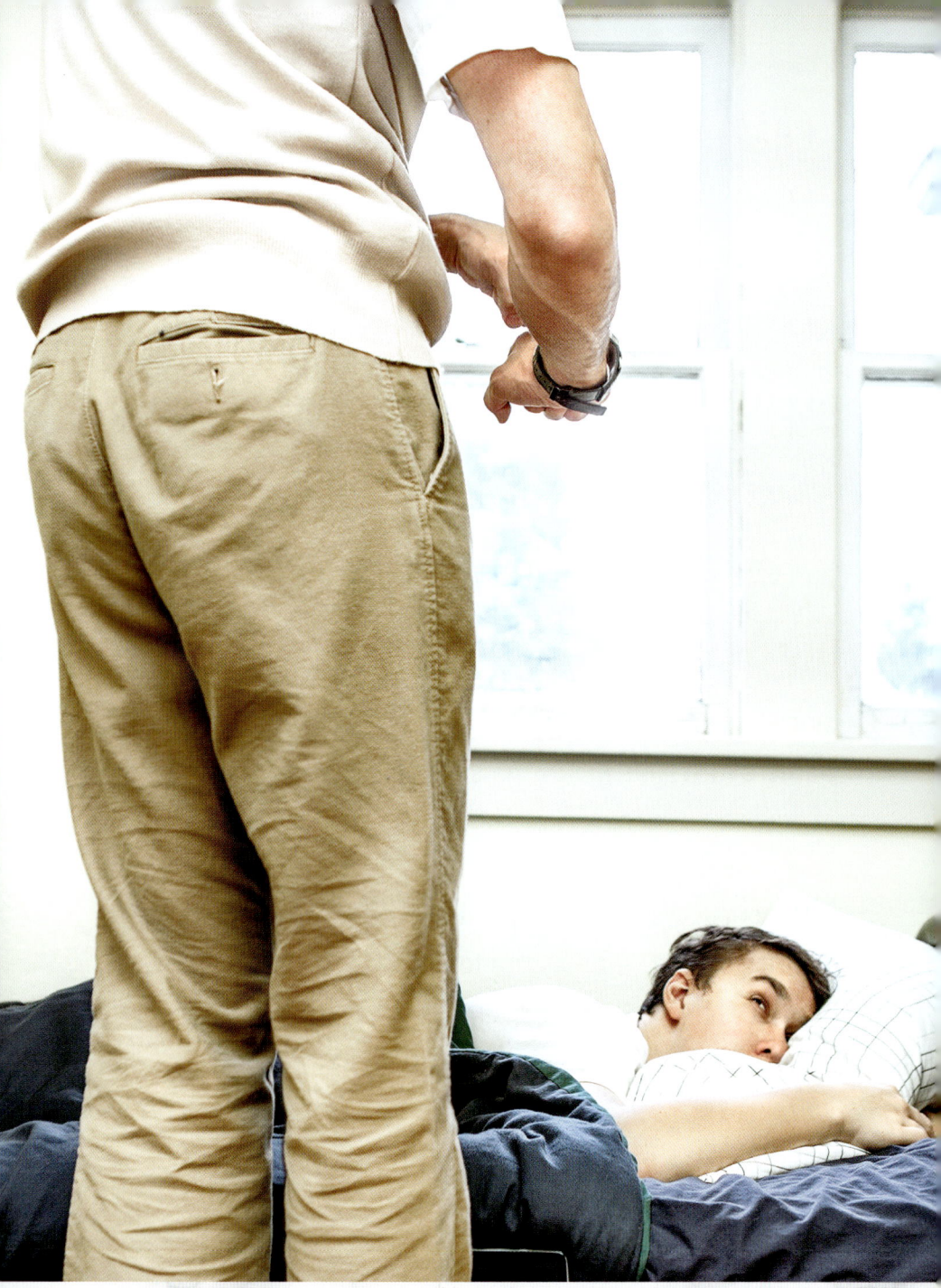

As teens go through puberty, they may experience increased conflict with their parents or caregivers.

CHAPTER ONE

FAMILIES, CONFLICT, AND CHANGE

Darnel heard a loud noise. He looked up from his phone to see his dad knocking on his bedroom doorframe. His dad looked mad, but that was nothing new. He got mad a lot since he lost his job a few months ago. It didn't help that Darnel's mom was more stressed too. Darnel's parents argued about money a lot. The sound of their lowered, angry voices rumbling through their closed bedroom door put knots in Darnel's stomach. What if his dad couldn't get another job? What if they had to move? What if his parents argued so much they got divorced?

Darnel took off his earbuds so he could hear his dad better. "What?" Darnel asked.

"You forgot to take out the trash," his dad said, frowning. "We aren't paying for trash service just so you can forget to take it out."

His dad's mouth continued to move, but Darnel couldn't hear him anymore. Blood rushed in his ears. Darnel felt like he never did anything right. He didn't mean to forget to take out the trash again. He just had a lot on his mind. Besides, was it such a big deal if the trash got picked up next week instead?

To his dad though, everything came down to money. Most days it felt like Darnel's parents cared more about money than they did about him. They never asked him how he was doing, or praised him for getting good grades, or noticed all the times he remembered his chores. Instead, they got mad when he bombed a test or forgot something.

Darnel's chest grew hot. His throat tightened. He was so sick of it! Finally, he burst out, "Why can't you just leave me alone for once!"

His dad's face turned red. "You can't talk to me like that, young man!"

Darnel got so mad that he pushed his dad out of the way and ran out of the house. He ran until his lungs burned. Then he slowed to a walk so he could breathe. Darnel knew he shouldn't have yelled at his dad. He felt lousy about it. He knew it was tough for his dad to be out of work. He knew his parents were trying their best. But Darnel wished his parents saw him and understood that life was challenging for him too.

When Darnel circled back to his house, his dad was outside waiting. He motioned Darnel over. He didn't look as mad as before. Darnel met his dad outside the garage doors.

"Sorry I forgot the trash," Darnel said.

His dad looked surprised. "Thank you, Darnel. And I'm sorry I lost my temper and yelled at you."

Now Darnel was surprised. "Yeah," he said. "Me too. I usually remember to take the trash out. I've got a lot on my mind lately."

Darnel's dad sighed. "I know you do. I forget that me being out of work is hard on all of us." He rolled a green trash can in front of Darnel. "How about this week you grab recycling, and I'll get the trash."

Darnel smiled. "OK."

FAMILY SUPPORT

Negotiating conflict and change at home requires large amounts of energy in the best of circumstances. Add the normal challenges of adolescence—academics and extracurricular activities, new romantic relationships, friendships, work, and college plans—and teens can quickly feel overwhelmed. During these years, teens' relationships with their families are also shifting. They may still look to their families for emotional and material support, but they also seek out other support systems in friends. They strive to establish independence from their caregivers.

Experts say that maintaining healthy family connections is key to help teens manage stress, as well as to help teens avoid depression and unhealthy coping strategies such as drug use and unprotected sex. Talking and spending time with a caring family member, even in the midst of change or conflict, can help teens mature into well-adjusted, caring adults.

Families are made up of one or more adults and often a child or children.

DEFINING FAMILY

The word *family* elicits different responses in people. For some, thoughts of family bring warm feelings of being cared for and supported. For others, thoughts of family conjure up chaotic, stressful, or even traumatic memories. Because all families have both strengths and weaknesses, most people's feelings about their families are mixed.

A family is a group of people united by marriage, blood, or adoption living in a single household. Blended families occur when parents remarry and combine their households, including children and stepchildren. Families sometimes share a household with extended family members, such as aunts, uncles, or cousins. In other cases, children are raised by extended family members such as grandparents.

A person's family of origin includes the caretakers and siblings that he or she grew up with. The caregivers who raise someone are that person's family of origin, regardless of whether they are related. A person's family of origin may also include siblings or other child relatives.

DIFFERENCES IN FAMILIES

A 2015 Pew Research Center study found that family sizes have decreased over time, partially because more women have entered the workforce. Less than half of mothers surveyed in 1975 were working, while three-quarters of mothers were employed full-time in 2015. In 1975, 40 percent of mothers had four or more children, which was a plurality of those surveyed. In 2015, only 14 percent of mothers had four or more children. The 2015 results also showed that compared to the 1975 participants, "a similar share (41 percent) of mothers" had two children.[1]

According to the 2015 survey, family structure varied greatly by race, age, and economic status. For example, white, Hispanic, and Asian American children were statistically more likely to live in two-parent households than Black children.[2] Additionally, the divorce rate had dropped among younger couples. According to an article in *Time* magazine, "Compared to their 2008 counterparts, young people in 2016 were 18 percent less likely to get divorced."[3] Two-parent households often were better off financially than single-parent households.

WHAT DO HEALTHY FAMILIES LOOK LIKE?

Teens may wonder whether their families are normal or healthy. Getting perspective on what healthy families look like can be tough. According to the National Domestic Violence Hotline, healthy families tend to talk about problems, be respectful to each other, and be honest with one another. Members of healthy families enjoy spending time together and apart, support one another, and have equal access to family resources.

Just because a family is stronger or weaker in some of these elements doesn't mean that the family structure is necessarily bad or unhealthy. Families who avoid conflict may have a hard time talking openly about problems or being honest. They also cannot resolve conflict if they avoid conflict entirely. Members can work together to improve the family's overall health by first recognizing their weaknesses and asking for help.

Early experiences within a family of origin strongly influence how a person operates in the world. Negative and traumatic childhood experiences and stressful conflicts can compromise a person's health and relationships in adulthood.

Alternatively, a person who receives nurture from caregivers, as well as tools to manage conflict and emotions, will take those skills into adult life. Children do not choose their families of origin, but their families of origin have significant, lasting impacts on their worldviews, their health, and their relationships.

HOW CHANGE LEADS TO FAMILY CONFLICT

While every family is different, all families experience some type of change over time. Families can plan for some changes, such as purchasing a new home or adopting a sibling. However, other changes may be unexpected, such as losing a job or going through a divorce. These changes can be temporary or permanent, and they may affect members of the family for the rest of their lives.

> "I AM THANKFUL FOR HAVING SUCH CANDID FAMILY MEMBERS TO ANSWER MY QUESTIONS. THEIR OPENNESS HELPED ME DEVELOP INTO THE PERSON I AM TODAY."[4]
> —ADRIAN, STUDENT

Change often leads to conflict. Conflict is when family members experience a clash of interests. They may disagree, debate, or fight to try to have their needs or desires met. Changes that are large, sudden, unexpected, or irreversible lead to the most intense conflicts. These conflicts can last for a few hours, for days, or even for years.

Each family member experiences conflict differently based on that person's perspective. For example, a parent might accept a new job that requires the family to move

Changes in friends, interests, or hobbies can all be sources of conflict among family members.

far away. The parent accepting the new job is likely to have a more positive view of the change than family members who do not have a say in the decision. Differences in perspective help explain why not all members of a family will have the same feelings about a shared experience. These differences alone can lead to conflict.

Divorces, births, deaths, financial difficulties, and moves create stress at home, where teens normally look for comfort. However, these events also provide teens with important opportunities to grow. Compromise, diplomacy, and speaking up for one's self are all essential skills developed while managing family change and conflict. Teens who master these skills are better prepared for college, careers, and their own families in the future.

ACCEPTING CHANGE

Uncertainty can be uncomfortable and feel scary. But accepting change and learning from it can lead to heightened resilience. Resilience is a person's ability to survive setbacks, failures, and tragedies. Psychologists have identified common factors of resilient people, including optimism, emotional regulation, and the ability to learn from change. According to psychologist Elyssa Barbash, a resilient person can gain many insights about his or her life while experiencing setbacks and hard times, which ultimately help a person grow. She stated:

> [Setbacks] are merely bumps in the road. . . . When you can look at these instances as just that, they don't hold as much power. This means you can free yourself from their occurrence, and you can continue to grow and change without allowing these moments and instances to hold you back.[5]

When parents get divorced, many aspects of the family's dynamic will shift. This can put strain on relationships.

CHAPTER TWO

COMMON FAMILY CHANGES

Although each family is different, many families face similar challenges. These challenges include becoming divorced or blended families, as well as changing family structure. Going through any change can strain relationships within a family, especially if some family members get caught in the middle of arguments or feel as if they need to take sides.

DIVORCED AND BLENDED FAMILIES

Statistics around divorce are murky, but experts believe that around 40 percent of all marriages in the United States end in divorce.[1] Reasons for divorce vary. The couple may decide they can no longer live together due to fighting, abuse, or addiction. One person in the marriage may fall in love with someone else. Sometimes there is no specific trigger, and the married people simply decide to go separate ways.

SIBLING RIVALRY

Perhaps no one can annoy teens as easily or as often as their siblings. In 2019, the average US family had 1.93 children.[3] That means most families had at least one child, and many had two or more.

Experts say that sibling rivalry is mostly due to competition over limited resources. This can include receiving attention from caregivers, having access to screen time, or taking the first shower before the hot water runs out. Experts also say siblings tend to fight more with siblings of their own gender and those closest to them in age.

As teens begin to establish their own unique identities, they may argue with siblings more. Families can help ease tension by implementing boundaries around individual resources such as belongings and personal space. Designating one-on-one time between caregivers and teens can also ease tensions.

Seventy-five percent of divorcees go on to remarry or start new relationships.[2] Many of these couples create new stepfamilies or blended families. Stepfamilies or blended families are formed when two adults and their children from previous relationships form a single household.

The first one to two years after becoming part of a blended family tend to be the most difficult time for teens. A teen may struggle to find her new role in a blended family. Blended families face unique conflicts. A child may feel torn between his new stepparent and his other caretaker. Stepfamilies may not share common histories, beliefs, or styles of relating.

Teens may also have to split their time between the homes of the caretakers in the prior relationship due to custody agreements. Building new bonds among stepfamily members that acknowledge these differences and challenges can take many years.

Teens whose parents have divorced may experience many emotions, including depression and anger. Teens may also worry that the divorce was their fault or that they could have done something to make their parents happy. However, it's important for teens to recognize that the unresolvable issues involved their parents and not them. Adjusting to life after divorce can be tough. Blended families often succeed with help from grandparents, therapists, clergy, and other community supports.

ECONOMIC HARDSHIP

Financial hardship is one of the most common difficulties faced by US families. Economic setbacks can come in many forms—job loss, unexpected medical or car repair bills, or even natural disasters. A 2015 study of 7,800 US households showed that 60 percent of those surveyed had experienced some kind of financial hardship in the previous year. One-third of those surveyed experienced two or more types of difficulties. And half of the families surveyed took six months or longer to recover from the latest financial setback.[4]

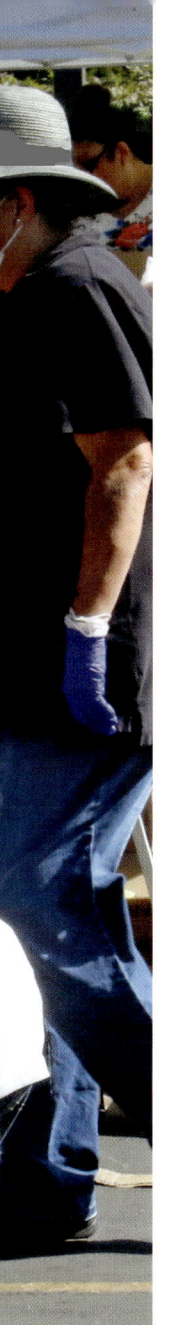

Families experiencing economic hardship may face homelessness, marriage instability, food shortages, and debt. Financial recovery can be a long, difficult road. In the meantime, teens and their families may struggle with not being able to make ends meet. Some teens may be expected to work to support their families. These teens are more likely to struggle with managing school expectations and social situations.

Families at all economic levels face financial hardships. However, low-income and single-parent households are hit hardest by unexpected bills. Caregivers in these households often don't have a lot of money saved. They have less of a financial buffer to support them during unexpected hardships.

Teens may feel a loss of control when their families experience ongoing or sudden financial hardship. They may also feel alone as their caregivers work long hours to pay bills and support the family. Teens may worry about their families' finances but find caregivers unwilling to talk about money. This can lead to frustration and anger.

During the COVID-19 global pandemic, many families who faced financial insecurity relied on food banks for their groceries.

JUGGLING RESPONSIBILITIES

Teens are often expected to fill in the gaps at home for busy, working caregivers. They may watch younger siblings or take on more household responsibilities. Some teens also work part-time jobs to help their families financially.

In 1979, nearly 60 percent of US teens were employed. In 2019, roughly 35 percent of teens were employed. However, today's teens actually have far less free time than their parents had.[6] Demands of a high school education are much higher in the 2020s than they were in previous decades, and teens often face additional expectations with volunteering and extracurricular activities.

Teens who are struggling to balance their responsibilities may feel overwhelmed. They may feel that their parents ask too much of them. One solution to feeling overwhelmed is to talk about these feelings with family members and caregivers. That way, the family can work together to help teens balance all of their responsibilities.

LOSS AND GRIEF

Five percent of children in the United States lose one or both parents before the age of 15.[5] Teens may also grieve the loss of a sibling, relative, or friend. Grief can last for weeks, months, or even years. While grieving, teens may have difficulty expressing their emotions. Grief does not always look like sadness. Grieving the loss of a loved one may also involve angry outbursts and feeling overwhelmed.

Teens experiencing grief may feel lonely or isolated. They may resent the lack of support they receive

The death of a family member or loved one can be difficult for a family to navigate.

from surviving family members who are also grieving. If the deceased person was responsible for financial support, teens may worry about how their family will handle economic challenges. Other aspects of grief may include a lack of focus, insomnia, and overeating or undereating.

Teens experiencing grief may engage in risky behavior, such as by taking drugs or driving recklessly. Grieving teens may also feel that the world is no longer a safe place and become anxious or hyperalert.

Teens may also develop a variety of healthy ways to cope with loss, according to a 2012 poll conducted by the National Alliance for Grieving Children. Teens who lost a significant loved one said that spending time with family members and talking with a caring adult helped them cope. Teens also reported that while talking to friends about a loss was difficult, they often felt supported when they did. Teens also used a variety of self-care techniques, such as listening to music and talking with other teens with similar loss experiences.

DOMESTIC ABUSE AND FAMILY VIOLENCE

Family violence and domestic abuse affect ten million people in the United States each year.[7] Abuse occurs when someone overpowers and harms another person physically, emotionally, verbally, or sexually. Domestic abuse is defined as violence within a home and generally refers to abuse among romantic or marital partners. However, family violence can also happen between siblings or between caregivers and children.

Neglect is another form of abuse. Neglect occurs when a caregiver fails to meet the basic needs of the children who are dependent on that caregiver. Emotional neglect happens when caregivers intentionally or unintentionally ignore a child's emotional needs. In either case, the victims of the abuse can suffer consequences for many years.

All forms of abuse go beyond healthy family conflict. Conflict is bound to happen in families, and family members can work through conflict together in healthy ways. But abuse is not a type of healthy conflict. Abuse and violence can follow teens into their adult relationships unless they get help with the trauma they have experienced.

TEEN PREGNANCY

According to data from the National Center for Health Statistics, in

GETTING HELP WITH ABUSE

In 2017, US government agencies determined that an estimated 674,000 children were victims of abuse.[8] Often, victims of abuse are afraid to speak out, so teens who are experiencing abuse may feel alone. Teens may blame themselves when, in fact, the abuse is not their fault. Abuse has serious physical, emotional, and psychological impacts on teens. Experiencing or witnessing abuse can lead to depression or substance use as a means to cope. For these reasons, it's important for teens to get help. Teens who are experiencing abuse, or who know of someone who is being abused, can contact the 24-hour, free, confidential Childhelp National Child Abuse Hotline. Teens can call or text 1-800-4-A-CHILD (1-800-422-4453) or visit childhelp.org/hotline.

2018 the teen pregnancy rate in the United States was a record low at less than half of what it was in 2008.[9] Experts believe the decrease may be due to teens not having sex as often and having better access to information and effective forms of contraception. However, teens may still find themselves responsible for raising children while they themselves are still growing up. Teen parents often depend on their families of origin for financial support, childcare, advice, and even shelter.

> "EVERYONE HAS A DIFFERENT VIEW ON HOW CHILDREN SHOULD BE RAISED, AND I LEARNED THAT YOU CAN'T PANIC—YOU JUST HAVE TO TRUST YOUR INSTINCTS IN THE END."[10]
>
> —PIPPA, TEEN MOM

Despite this dependence, teen parents' views will inevitably conflict with those of their own parents. Teens may want to create different family dynamics than the ones in which they were raised. They may learn new approaches and techniques to parenting that weren't available to their parents. Meanwhile, teens' parents may struggle to recognize their teens' newfound maturity. They may want to share their parenting experiences but end up overstepping or interfering with their teens' choices in child-rearing. Positive, supportive relationships between teen parents and their families of origin can offer a stable, lasting influence in a child's life for years to come. Ongoing communication and healthy boundaries are key to resolving these differences.

ADDICTION

Whether teens, their caregivers, or their siblings are the ones abusing drugs or alcohol, addiction disrupts a family's dynamic and introduces incredible amounts of stress and conflict. It also impairs a family's finances as well as family members' physical, emotional, and psychological health. Children of caregivers who suffer from addiction often experience a lot of conflict. According to the American Academy of Child and Adolescent Psychiatry (AACAP), one in five American adults lived with an alcoholic relative as a child. These individuals are at a greater risk for behavioral and emotional difficulties. Children of parents suffering from alcoholism are also four times as likely to develop substance abuse issues

> "WHEN BEHAVIORS TAKE ON THE FORM OF A PATTERN, THEY MAY BE MORE HABITUAL AND HARDER TO CHANGE. THIS DOES NOT MEAN IT IS IMPOSSIBLE, BUT IT DOES REQUIRE YOU TO HAVE PATIENCE WITH YOUR PARENT OR GUARDIAN, AS NO ONE IS PERFECT AT MODIFYING HIS OR HER CONDUCT IMMEDIATELY."[11]
>
> —TALIA, 22

themselves, and they may develop relationships with partners who experience substance abuse issues as adults.[12]

Addiction recovery is a process that can often involve the participation of the entire family. It's important for those suffering from addiction and for their family members to get help. Organizations such as Alcoholics Anonymous, Alateen, and Narcotics Anonymous provide support for those people and their families.

These are just a few examples of the most common kinds of conflicts and changes teens may experience in their families. Teens may find these challenges reflected in their own lives or in the lives of their friends and neighbors. Which challenges teens are likely to face and how their families address those conflicts depend on a variety of factors.

A parent struggling with alcoholism may not be able to support other members of the family. This may cause children to grow up faster in order to "parent" their parents.

Siblings' relationships change as they grow up. Sometimes siblings are close, while others do not speak to one another.

CHAPTER THREE

FAMILY DYNAMICS

Change can lead to conflict in families. How families cope with conflict depends on family dynamics, such as social structure, relational style, and family history. Additional sociological factors such as race, economic status, and religion also factor into the types and intensities of conflicts families face. The family's culture also plays an important role.

ELEMENTS OF FAMILY DYNAMICS

Family dynamics are the patterns of how family members relate to and interact with one another and with those outside the family. These can involve how teens relate to themselves, their siblings, or their parents. Family dynamics can also be about how open or closed members are to those outside the family.

One aspect in determining family dynamics is social structure. Social structure refers to whether a family is more hierarchical, a situation in which the parents have most of the power, or egalitarian, a situation in which all members of the family have voices. An egalitarian

CLASS AND FAMILY STABILITY

The United States is increasingly divided along socioeconomic lines when it comes to marriage and family stability. Couples with higher incomes are more likely to enjoy strong, stable marriages, which are linked with social and economic benefits, such as homeownership. Meanwhile, low-income and working-class families face greater instability due to higher rates of single parenthood and divorce. The instability negatively affects families economically, psychologically, and socially. Experts say this disparity is due to cultural and economic changes that have disproportionately affected low-income and working-class families.

family may discuss conflicts openly. A more hierarchical family will expect members to follow the wishes of the head of the family.

According to family systems theory, psychologists and researchers may also view families by how members relate to those inside and outside the family system. Families may fall on a continuum from open to closed, or they may be random. Closed families are less influenced by outside input. They tend to value structure, rules, privacy, and discipline, and they may have high expectations for members' behavior and achievement. Open families value emotional connection, tend to be more casual and open to outsiders, and emphasize cooperation. Random families recognize that no one style will meet the needs of all individual members and emphasize exploration through personal intuition and creativity.

A family's history is perhaps one of the most important factors in determining dynamics. Difficulties such as divorce, serious illness, addiction, or financial hardship directly affect how much stamina family members have for resolving daily conflicts. Likewise, difficulties faced by previous generations can affect how members relate to one another in the present. For example, people raised in dysfunctional or abusive homes may have to work harder to develop healthy parenting skills for use with their own children.

PROBLEMATIC FAMILY ROLES AND FUNCTIONS

Families can get stuck in roles and functions that limit their abilities to resolve conflict. For instance, a teen whose parents often fight can become the family peacekeeper in an effort to keep everyone together. One parent might choose to communicate issues with another parent to the child, rather than talk to the other parent. A young person with different ideologies from those of her or his caregivers or a history of troublemaking may end up feeling ostracized from the rest of the family. Families will sometimes focus on one member's addiction or mental illness as a way to avoid dealing with other relational issues. Other families may form alignments along gender roles, pitting female and male members against one another. These roles hurt family members' self-esteem, weaken bonds, and limit their abilities to resolve conflicts. Families can work together and with family therapists to identify patterns and roles that no longer serve them well. They can then develop healthier ways of relating, such as active communication.

THE SOCIOLOGY OF FAMILIES AND CONFLICT

Families are also affected by sociological factors, such as race, socioeconomic status, and religion. According to the American Academy of Pediatrics (AAP), teens from ethnic and racial minorities may experience challenges not faced by their white peers, or they may experience some challenges more intensely because of racism. For example, youth from African American, Hispanic, and American Indian families are more likely to be incarcerated than their white peers. According to data from the US Bureau of Labor Statistics, unemployment rates among African American men have been consistently double those of white men since 1972. Also, African American men tend to get paid less, earning approximately 72 percent of what white men earn, which creates an economic burden for their families.[1]

> "BEING AN IMMIGRANT HAS BEEN HARD, BUT IT HAS TAUGHT ME THAT NO MATTER WHERE IN THE WORLD I AM, I SHOULD LEARN TO RESPECT OTHER PEOPLE'S DIFFERENCES."[3]
>
> —NEEMA, 17

Immigrant families may experience discrimination while also clashing over cultural values. More than 44.7 million immigrants lived in the United States in 2018.[2] Immigrant

Children of immigrant parents may have different opinions than their parents because the children's opinions are based in the culture of their new country.

parents may try to pass on their traditions and beliefs to their children, while the younger generation may adapt to the expectations of mainstream American culture and their peers. This can create a conflict between generations.

Families are also affected by their socioeconomic status (SES), which is determined by a number of complex factors including income, education, and occupation. When compared to high SES families, low SES families are more likely to experience depression, addiction, and obesity. Low SES families have fewer resources to recover from negative changes and setbacks, such as job loss and health problems. Low SES families are also more likely to experience divorce and family instability.

Finally, families whose members share a common faith may rely on religious communities for support. Religious communities can offer financial assistance, emotional support, and advice in addressing moral and spiritual issues. However, teens may reject their families' beliefs as they develop separate identities, which creates ideological conflicts with their caregivers.

FAMILIES AND FAITH

Faith can play a vital, supportive role in families. Most organized religions advocate for responsible parenting and strong family relationships. Family members bond through shared activities and traditions, and they create strong social ties within a larger community. However, religion can also create friction in a home. During adolescence, teens question all forms of authority, including spiritual authority. Teens may resist conforming to their parents' beliefs and form ideologies of their own. Some parents will be more tolerant of a teen's beliefs and open to hearing a teen's perspective. Other parents will insist on teens following the family's traditions as long as they're living at home. A healthy compromise regarding faith differences makes room for both the family's values and the teen's sense of self.

CULTURAL APPROACHES TO FAMILY CONFLICT

Families are also influenced by the expectations and biases of the dominant culture in which they live, as well as their historical cultures. These factors affect how families operate and how they approach conflict.

For instance, a study conducted by the Frances McClelland Institute for Children, Youth, and Families explored the differences between white and Asian American families. Researchers found that US families from European backgrounds tend to value authoritative styles of parenting. This parenting style emphasizes individuality and provides moderate limitations on children's behaviors. Many Asian American families, however, prefer an authoritarian

MIXED-STATUS FAMILIES

In 2019, the Pew Research Center estimated that 10.5 million undocumented immigrants lived in the United States in 2017.[4] Many immigrants lived in mixed-status families, in which members have different immigration statuses. According to the Migration Policy Institute, in 2016, 37 percent of undocumented immigrants lived with children younger than 18. Of these children, 80 percent were US citizens.[5]

Mixed-status families face unique challenges, including a higher risk of poverty. Undocumented parents can face precarious job situations. They may be reluctant to access programs and services, such as food assistance or government health insurance, due to fear of deportation.

Poverty and fear of deportation can take a toll on mixed-status families. Teens in these families may feel as if they are living in the shadows. The stress affects their mental and physical health, their academic opportunities, and the family's ability to manage conflict and change.

Although parenting styles may differ, all families can have fun while spending time together.

approach. With an authoritarian approach, parents exercise high levels of control over their children's lives while emphasizing duty to family and culture.

Additionally, parenting styles may differ among racial or ethnic groups due to differences in goals for their children. For example, a 2015 Pew Research study showed that "while similar shares of Black and white parents say it is extremely important to them for their children to grow up to be honest and ethical and caring and compassionate, Black parents place more value than white parents on raising their kids to be hardworking, ambitious and financially independent."[6]

Researchers found that while authoritarian and authoritative approaches differ, one is not necessarily more beneficial to children than the other. Both approaches use different degrees of warmth, control, and parental sacrifice to protect children and offer an environment that helps them to succeed. Each approach also determines the types of conflicts family members are likely to face and how those conflicts are resolved.

> "THERE ARE TIMES WHEN IT IS IN YOUR BEST INTERESTS TO LISTEN TO YOUR PARENT. WHEN YOU DO THIS YOU HAVE TO KNOW THE DIFFERENCE BETWEEN HEARING AND LISTENING."[7]
>
> —RAUL, 17

Teens gain independence during adolescence, but this can create a need for healthy conflict resolution within the family.

CHAPTER FOUR

ADOLESCENCE AND FAMILY CONFLICT

As children develop into teenagers, they are more likely to experience an increase in conflict with their families of origin. Change can be one reason for this conflict. However, there are many causes of conflict, including puberty.

At the onset of puberty, sex hormones that have been present since birth surge. Puberty occurs when a person's sexual organs mature and become capable of producing offspring. The average age to reach puberty is between eight and 14 years old, depending on a child's sex. After puberty, teens experience strong fluctuations in hormones. As their brains adapt to these changes, teens can experience an increase in irritability and aggression. This is not to say that raging hormones or moodiness cause all conflicts between teens and their families. However, it can be helpful to recognize that brain chemistry plays an important role in the increase of conflict between teens and caregivers during these years.

Developmentally, teenagers are also growing separate from and independent of their caregivers, a process known as individuating. Teens begin to define their identities—who they are and what they stand for—apart from those of their families of origin. During individuation, teens may reject their caregivers' standards, values, or viewpoints.

Caregivers, on the other hand, may struggle to recognize that their teenagers aren't younger versions of themselves. Instead, each teen is her own unique mosaic of personality, experiences, talents, and interests. Caregivers may take their teens' rejection personally.

ASKING CAREGIVERS FOR HELP

Giving and receiving help is an important part of family relationships. However, for teens, asking for help isn't always as easy as it sounds. Teens are working to develop independence from their caregivers. This may lead them to feel that asking for help is a sign of weakness or failure. Adults also may not realize their teens need help. They may be focused on their own concerns and fail to recognize when teens are struggling. Teens may also pretend that things are fine because they don't want to add to their parents' stress.

However, knowing what one needs and asking for help indicates maturity and confidence. Accepting help also strengthens the relationship between teens and their families and increases feelings of safety and connection. Asking for and receiving help is a healthy step for everyone in a family.

CONFLICT AND STAGES OF ADOLESCENCE

Adolescence is the period of time between childhood and adulthood. It is generally separated into early, middle, and late stages. Teens may relate differently to their families as they develop, mature, and progress through each stage.

Early adolescence occurs between the ages of ten and 13. Children in this phase have concrete, black-and-white thinking that makes it difficult for them to see other family members' points of view. They may also have an increased desire for privacy, which can create conflict with caregivers and siblings.

Middle adolescence occurs between the ages of 14 and 17. Teens may begin to enter romantic relationships and explore their sexual identities. These changes can be especially stressful

> "PARENTAL CONTROL CERTAINLY MATTERS; PARENTAL COMMUNICATION MATTERS MORE."[1]
> —CARL E. PICKHARDT, PSYCHOLOGIST

if they lack family support. Middle adolescents tend to start arguing more with their parents as they struggle for independence. They may spend less time with family and more with their peers. Middle adolescents are improving their abilities to think abstractly. However, they may still struggle to make complex decisions and control

MAKING HEALTHY CHOICES AROUND SEX

Deciding when to have sex is a big choice for teens. The right time to start having sex is different for everyone. Deciding to have sex is a choice teens should make after careful consideration and preparation.

Parents may feel their teens aren't ready to become sexually active. Parents may also have religious views about sex that their teens may or may not share. However, talking to a trusted adult, such as a parent, is generally a positive first step for a teen deciding to have sex for the first time.

A teen who is considering becoming sexually active should also consider a few important points. Unprotected sex comes with risks of sexually transmitted infections (STIs) and unintended pregnancy. Sex should be with a partner the teen trusts and respects, and it should be with consent that is freely and enthusiastically given. And teens shouldn't engage in sex until they are ready for the emotional and physical outcomes of sexual intimacy.

their impulses. This is because the brain continues to develop until a person is in her or his twenties. Strong emotions tend to drive decision-making.

Late adolescence, or emerging adulthood, is a developmental stage that occurs between the ages of 18 and 25. People in this stage have finished developing physically, though their brains may not fully develop until age 25. They have usually improved their abilities for impulse control and may gauge risks and outcomes more accurately than when they were younger. Late adolescents also tend to have strong senses

Many teens enter romantic relationships for the first time. They may want to spend more time with their partners than with their caregivers.

of self and their own values. They are often physically and emotionally separate from their families. At this stage, adolescents' relationships with their parents may shift into more equal, adult friendships. They may find themselves asking for advice from caregivers they rebelled against just a few years earlier.

THE IMPACT OF STRESS ON TEENS

Stress also leads to conflict between teens and their families. External factors such as financial struggles,

One way to reduce stress is to participate in light exercise, such as swimming or yoga.

health or marriage problems, and social adversity can lead to increased stress for all family members. Caregivers who experience these hardships may be irritable, weary, and distracted. They may fail to follow through on promises they make or behave inconsistently.

However, stress affects teens as well. In response to stress, the brain releases the steroid allopregnanolone, also known as THP. In adults, THP helps regulate anxiety. In teens however, THP has the opposite effect, causing teens to feel more easily overwhelmed and anxious.

While THP is just one physiological response to stress, it highlights the differences between how teens and adults respond to stress.

Adults may also have developed perspective and healthy coping mechanisms for anxiety and stress throughout their lives. Teens have not yet had that opportunity. As a result, teens are much more likely than adults to exhibit stress-induced illnesses and habits. When their home lives are filled with conflict, teens can feel trapped and unsupported.

Teens may feel tempted to use raging hormones as an excuse to lash out or make

STRESS MANAGEMENT SKILLS FOR TEENS

In a survey conducted by the American Psychological Association (APA), 31 percent of teens reported feeling overwhelmed due to stress in the past month.[2] Commonly reported triggers included school, choices about the future, and concerns about finances. Other triggers included not eating or sleeping enough, difficult relationships, or an overloaded schedule.

Since symptoms of stress often mimic normal teenage experiences, stress can sneak up on teens. Symptoms of significant stress include an increase in feelings of depression or anxiety, headaches or stomachaches, changes in appetite or the ability to sleep, and difficulty concentrating. Teens can cope with stress by first recognizing that they are struggling and then asking for help. Teens can talk to a caregiver or another trusted adult. They can also develop stress-management strategies, such as eating and exercising regularly, practicing relaxation techniques, and building a support network of friends.

TEENS IN FOSTER CARE

In 2020, more than 442,000 children were in foster care, according to the National Conference of State Legislatures. A quarter of those children were aged 14 or older.[3] Teens are placed in foster care when their legal caregivers are unable to adequately meet the teens' physical and emotional needs. These teens may have experienced abuse or neglect as well as chronic conflict and instability. To enter foster care, teens may leave behind everything familiar—home, family, school, friends, and neighborhoods. They live with a high level of uncertainty about their futures. Will they return home? Will they be adopted?

There is no one right way to navigate foster care. Teens need the support of a team to succeed, including social workers, relatives, foster parents, therapists, and friends. Foster care advocacy groups such as FosterClub and *Represent* magazine also provide resources to help foster care teens connect and take control of their futures.

poor choices. Similarly, caregivers may dismiss teens' desires and views as developmental phases. Neither is accurate or fair. Instead, teens and caregivers can work together to develop a family environment that offers perspective, support, and accountability while meeting teens' needs.

DEVELOPING RESILIENCE

Having a sense of control can be reassuring. Factors such as brain chemistry, physical development, and changes to family structure, however, are outside of teens' control. This loss of control can lead to feelings of anxiety and fear. Instead of looking for ways to control their environments, the American Psychological Association (APA) states that teens can work to develop resilience.

Resilience is the ability to adapt successfully in the face of change and conflict. Teens who are resilient seem to roll with the punches. According to the APA, resilience is a skill teens can learn through experience. It is not a skill or trait that someone has naturally. Instead, resilience is a process that develops over time, and one that can be honed through practice.

Teens who are resilient share common traits. They are connected with a supportive community of friends and family. Resilient teens take care of themselves physically and mentally. They know how to ask for help, and they are able to see the big picture. Resilient teens still experience stress and feel anxious. However, developing resilience helps teens bounce back and move on from life's challenges.

> "HEALTHY AND PRODUCTIVE CONVERSATIONS NEED TO GO BOTH WAYS. IN ADVOCATING FOR OURSELVES, WE NEED TO MAKE SPACE FOR OTHER PEOPLE TO QUESTION OR DISAGREE."[4]
> —GABY, 19

Some forms of conflict resolution, such as avoiding or ignoring another person, are considered unhealthy.

CHAPTER FIVE

TYPES OF FAMILY CONFLICT

While conflict is a normal part of relationships, not all forms of conflict are constructive or healthy, and some are even harmful. Likewise, while families may differ on how they approach conflict, some approaches are more effective than others. Understanding the difference can help teens make choices around conflict that keep them safe and better connect them with their families.

RECOGNIZING UNHEALTHY CONFLICT

Conflict ceases to be constructive when people stop making conscious choices about their words and actions or when they make conscious choices to use destructive or hurtful behaviors. Signs of unhealthy conflict include someone becoming intensely angry, yelling, lunging toward or otherwise threatening the other person, using demeaning language, or being physically abusive. However, they may also be more covert. These tactics

SETTING FAMILY BOUNDARIES

Setting boundaries helps family members agree on what are reasonable, safe, and permissible behaviors. Families can also set boundaries on how to respond if someone steps outside those expectations. Boundaries create safety and trust within a family. Boundaries protect physical space. For example, a rule might be that family members don't hit one another. Boundaries preserve emotional well-being. For example, family members might agree not to use hurtful language. Boundaries can also be intellectual. Intellectual boundaries recognize members' opinions, views, and beliefs.

Teens may set their own boundaries within their families. A reasonable boundary is a request for a change in behavior, such as, "Please knock before entering my room." Learning to set healthy boundaries takes time. Boundaries should be communicated clearly, calmly, and without apology. Setting boundaries may feel selfish, but boundaries are necessary parts of self-care and healthy relationships.

include avoiding and withdrawing from conflict or using nonverbal hostility such as rolling eyes, sighing, or giving someone the silent treatment.

While it may be tempting to match a person's explosive energy, this rarely leads to positive outcomes. Instead of saying or doing something they later regret, both people in a conflict can take a break. They can return to the conversation when they're calm.

Conflict is unhealthy when it creates sustained or chronic stress for family members. Stress hormones, such as cortisol and adrenaline,

Siblings who fight and argue often may find it difficult to try healthy conflict-resolution techniques.

prepare teens' bodies to face emergencies. However, when teens experience sustained stress, their bodies' emergency response systems run continuously, creating health risks. Teens who experience chronic stress from conflict are at an increased risk for depression, high blood pressure, and type 2 diabetes.

Continuous upheaval that creates chronic stress is unhelpful and unhealthy. Teens may not be able to control

ASSERTIVE VS. AGGRESSIVE

Teens can communicate their needs through assertiveness or through aggression. Aggression is often rooted in low self-esteem and feelings of powerlessness. Thus, aggressive communication resorts to physical and emotional intimidation and dominance in order to get one's way. It also expresses feelings and views in a way that is disrespectful to others. Aggressive people may seem to care only about their own needs. They are quick to blame others and avoid taking responsibility. As a result, they often alienate themselves.

On the other hand, assertive teens advocate for their own needs respectfully. Assertiveness is a direct, respectful form of communication. These teens communicate in a clear, calm manner. Assertive teens use nonthreatening words and body language. They don't let their feelings get the best of them. They stand up for themselves. When teens use assertive communication, others are more likely to feel respected and better understand their needs.

or eliminate conflict. However, it is important for them to ask for the help of trusted adults and to take care of themselves in the midst of the chaos.

INEFFECTIVE APPROACHES TO CONFLICT

Families may use a variety of approaches to deal with conflict, but not all approaches are skillful. Unskillful approaches are those that are unhelpful and either mask the problem or avoid addressing it entirely. They may even create additional problems.

One common example of an unskillful

approach to conflict is passive aggression. Though often difficult to recognize, passive aggression is a deliberate but masked way of expressing anger. A person acting passive-aggressively will avoid the conflict by appearing to go along with another person's demands. Meanwhile, the person will behave negatively or covertly resist. The person may also deny his or her behavior, all the while refusing to cooperate.

> "IF YOU SET YOUR OWN BOUNDARIES AND HAVE RELATIONSHIPS WITH PEOPLE WHO RESPECT YOUR BOUNDARIES, YOU FEEL EMPOWERED TO DO WHAT YOU FEEL IS RIGHT."[1]
> —CASANDRA, 18

Families may also resort to defensiveness during conflicts. Instead of addressing a person's concerns, defensive family members may steadfastly deny any wrongdoing. Denying responsibility leads to other family members feeling unheard. Defensive family members may also shift blame to others in an attempt to avoid taking responsibility. They may criticize others to avoid addressing their own actions.

Other unskillful approaches families may make when facing conflict include refusing to compromise or to see another person's perspective. Family members may see the conflict as a win-lose scenario in which they are afraid to lose. They may also withdraw their affection or attention from other family members in an attempt to shame them into complying with their wishes.

None of these approaches is skillful or will lead to resolving conflict. In fact, they often lead to further hurt feelings and misunderstandings. In order to find a resolution, it's important for family members to first understand what healthy conflict looks like.

SKILLFUL FAMILY CONFLICT

Conflict arises whenever family members disagree over their values, desires, opinions, motivations, or ideas. Conflict triggers strong emotional responses and can lead to hard feelings. When handled unskillfully, conflict can damage family members' relationships and individuals' well-being. When handled in a healthy, skillful way, conflict actually improves and strengthens relationships and builds understanding and trust. Skillful conflict is based on empathy and respect. Family members recognize that someone's unmet need is at the

> One form of healthy conflict resolution is using active listening, or making sure to fully listen to what someone has to say before adding to the conversation.

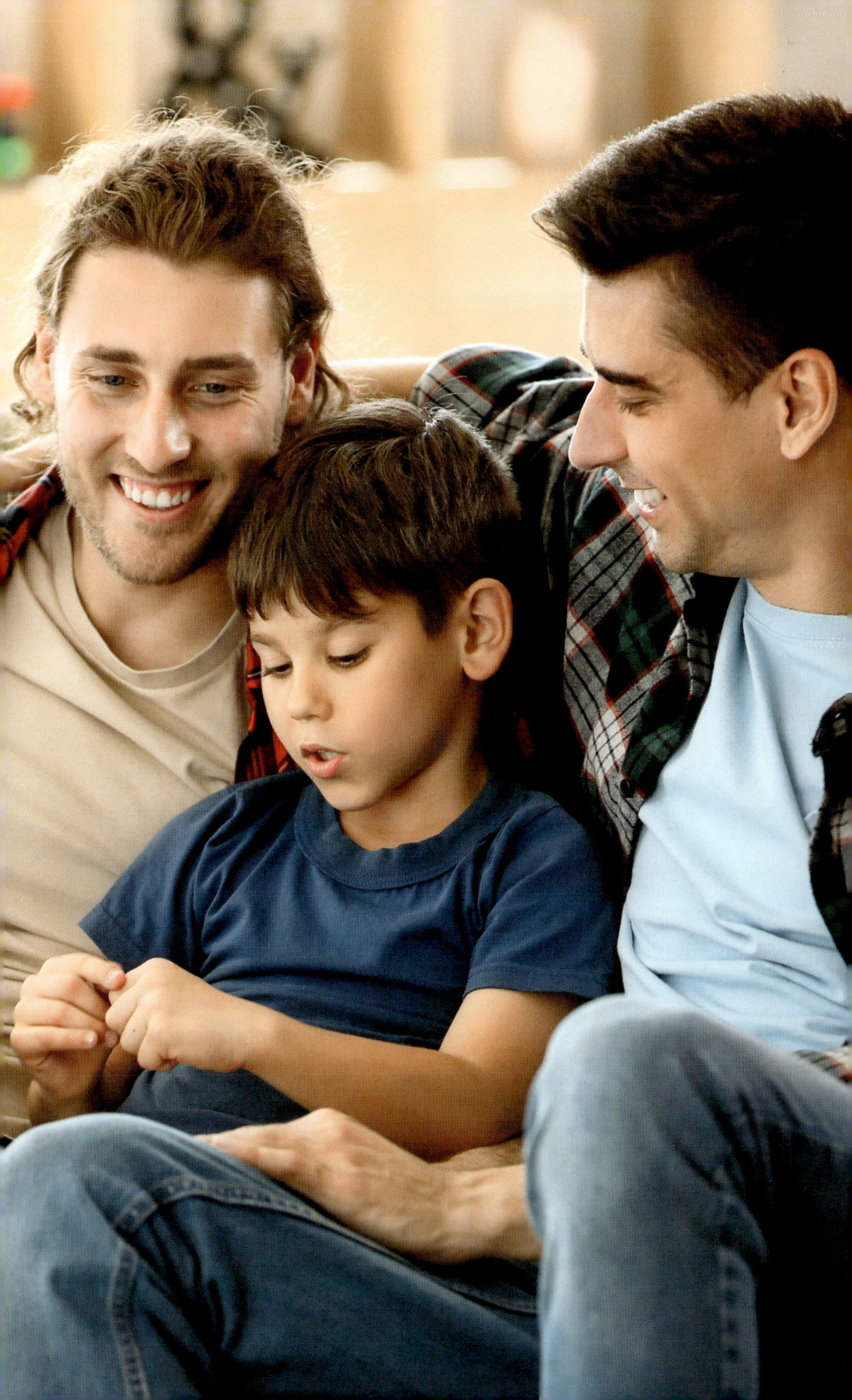

BUILDING A HEALTHY FAMILY

Many teens wonder whether their families are healthy. According to healthychildren.org, a site sponsored by the AAP, all families are different, but well-functioning families often share several broad traits. These traits include affection, a sense of belonging, stability, and open communication. In healthy families, all members feel respected and valued.

Families who want to grow closer can start by spending time together. They can share meals, hobbies, and interests. Families also benefit from predictable daily routines and shared traditions. One way a person can reduce stress is by asking for help instead of always trying to handle problems alone. Other family members can be available to help. Staying connected with relatives or communities also offers families security and support. Teens can start with themselves by developing a self-care routine, including adequate nutrition and sleep.

heart of the conflict. They make an effort to see that person's point of view, even if they don't share it.

Families with skillful conflict approaches avoid being defensive or confrontational. Instead, they strike a balance between speaking and listening. Family members focus on improving communication and finding a solution, not on scoring points. Skillful conflict addresses issues as they come up. Family members don't wait for problems to fester. They look for compromises when possible. Also, skillful conflict allows family members to set aside hard feelings and move on. Family members don't stay angry or resentful, because their needs have been met.

Families who use skillful approaches to conflict also manage their emotions well. Instead of denying or ignoring their feelings, they tend to face and express feelings. Family members are able to stay calm and take breaks when emotions run hot. Once they're calm again, they return to the topic instead of burying the problem.

Additionally, family members understand that developing skillful approaches to conflict takes time and practice. They don't expect to

BE A SCIENTIST, NOT A JUDGE

Teens may judge themselves harshly for feeling emotions they deem inappropriate, or they may assume they know how someone else feels based on that person's actions or facial expressions. However, psychologists say that these assumptions about other people's feelings are often incorrect. Misreading others' emotions can lead to unhelpful responses. And judging one's own emotions is unhelpful and only adds to the teen's stress.

Marc Brackett, director of the Yale Center for Emotional Intelligence, recommends that instead of judging emotions, teens take on the mindset of an "emotional scientist."[2] Scientists are curious. They do not make assumptions or harsh judgments. Instead, scientists ask questions. They look for causes and solutions. Becoming scientists of emotion in their families is one way teens can resolve conflicts with other family members in healthy, constructive ways.

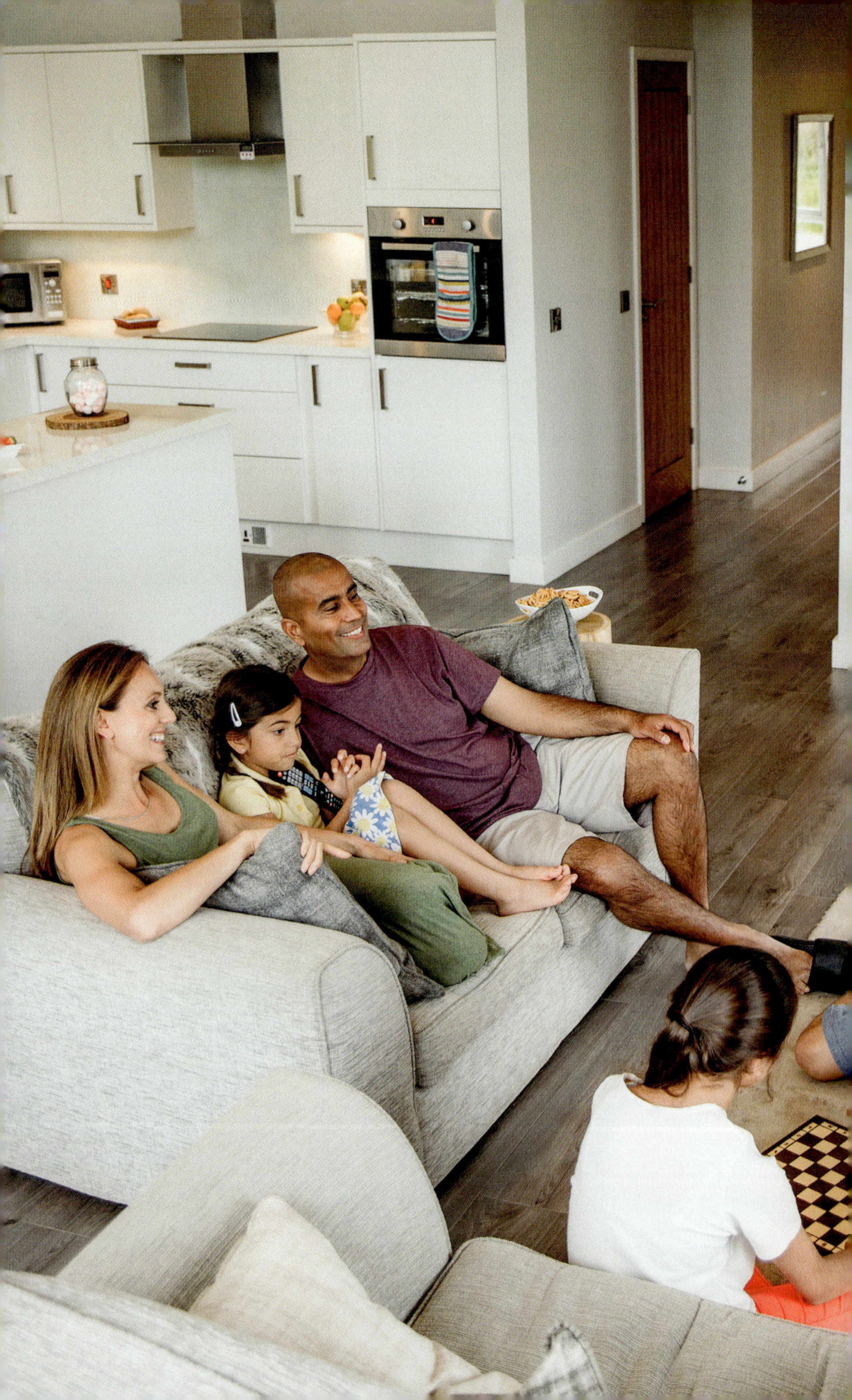

get it right the first time. They are patient with themselves and each other. They also understand that true family harmony comes when conflicts are resolved. These families appreciate that, although it can be difficult, facing conflict in a skillful way strengthens their relationships. Families who are able to master skillful approaches to conflict will enjoy a greater sense of trust and security and be better able to weather the challenges and changes of life.

Families who spend time together may develop better conflict-resolution skills.

One symptom of PTSD is recurring nightmares.

CHAPTER SIX

CONFLICT AND TRAUMA

While all traumatic experiences are stressful, not all stress is traumatic. Trauma is a response to a distressing, overwhelming event. Teens who experience trauma may feel helpless and numb to their own emotions. They may suffer from nightmares, be easily startled, or always feel alert for danger. These symptoms may continue well after a trauma occurs.

Teens who experience trauma may develop post-traumatic stress disorder (PTSD). Victims of abuse or sexual assault, war veterans, and others can develop PTSD. Symptoms include emotional distress, insomnia, flashbacks, panic attacks, and anxiety or depression. Untreated PTSD symptoms may be so severe that they lead some to have suicidal thoughts.

Because their brains are still developing, children and teens are especially susceptible to the effects of trauma. When trauma occurs, regions of the brain responsible for fear and anxiety may overproduce neural connections. This leads to a habitual fear response and hyperalertness even when the environment is stable and safe. Meanwhile,

CHILDHOOD TOXIC STRESS

Many communities who have a high exposure to adverse childhood experiences (ACEs) are also at higher risk for additional stressors, such as childhood toxic stress. This occurs when people younger than 18 experience severe, prolonged, or repetitive stressors without the nurture or support of caregivers. These stressors may include neighborhood violence, homelessness, and racism.

The toxic stress response in teens' bodies can be compared to revving the engine of a car for days or weeks at a time. Eventually, the car's mechanical parts show significant wear and tear, and the car fails to function properly. Likewise, as teens grow into adults, their bodies can become ill due to prolonged stress. When caregivers fail to meet the emotional or physical needs of a child, the teen's ability to cope with and recover from ACEs is reduced.

the parts of the brain dedicated to learning, rational thinking, and impulse control create fewer neural connections. This loss could lead to learning impairments, addictions, and behavioral problems.

ADVERSE CHILDHOOD EXPERIENCES

From 1995 to 1997, the US Centers for Disease Control and Prevention (CDC) and Kaiser Permanente, a health-care company, conducted the Adverse Childhood Experiences (ACEs) Study. It was conducted through confidential surveys of more than 17,000 Kaiser Permanente patients.[1]

The study investigated the link between ten ACEs—such as physical and emotional abuse, neglect, household violence, or mental illness of a caregiver—and medical, mental, and social outcomes later in life. The study showed that ACEs affect children's health and well-being as adults. The study also changed how public health experts understood human development. The more ACEs a child experiences, the higher his or her score. Children with several ACEs are at greater risk for developing health concerns such as heart disease, cancer, and diabetes than their peers with fewer ACEs. They are also at increased risk for attempted suicide, addiction, and becoming involved in abusive adult relationships.

> "INQUIRE, GO DEEP INTO YOURSELF, AND CLARIFY WHAT THE CONFLICT IS REALLY ABOUT. . . . CHANCES ARE THAT WHILE THE FIGHT IS ABOUT A SPECIFIC ISSUE, IN REALITY, YOU ARE AFTER SOMETHING THAT LIES AT A DEEPER LEVEL."[2]
>
> —ALDO CIVICO, CONFLICT RESOLUTION EXPERT

A prominent study found that ACEs are very common in the United States. Sixty-two percent of adults surveyed reported experiencing at least one ACE. However, people surveyed rarely experienced just one type of trauma. In fact, 87 percent of adults who reported trauma

POST-TRAUMATIC GROWTH

The field of positive psychology has noted the process of self-improvement that can follow trauma. This is called post-traumatic growth, or PTG. Between 30 and 70 percent of those who experience trauma report positive personal growth from their experiences.[5] These PTG survivors are able to develop a strengths-based perspective that helps them thrive and even go on to help others.

Experts studying PTG found several commonalities in survivors. PTG survivors reported experiencing supportive relationships in which they felt accepted. PTG survivors also shared two traits: openness to experience and extroversion. People with these traits are more likely to seek out social connection and to be willing to reconsider old self-perceptions. PTG experts advise trauma survivors not to minimize their pain or attempt to jump right into growth, however. PTG comes with time and patience.

experienced two or more ACEs.[3] The most commonly reported ACEs were economic hardship and divorce.

Twelve percent of those surveyed reported experiencing four or more ACEs. These adults were in the greatest risk category. Adults who reported experiencing four or more ACEs were almost four times likelier to get pulmonary lung disease. They were more than four times likelier to face depression and more than 12 times likelier to have attempted suicide.[4]

ACE AND SES

Strong evidence shows that families facing financial hardships are at

If a parent or caregiver loses his job, that may lead to children in the family experiencing more ACEs.

the greatest risk for ACE exposures, which may help explain why ACEs are so prevalent. According to the CDC, nearly one in ten children in the United States live in deep poverty, with their families earning below 50 percent of the poverty threshold. Four out of ten children live in low-income households that struggle to make ends meet.[6]

Teens in low-income families may be exposed to more ACEs for several reasons. Parents in low-income families

CAN TRAUMA BE INHERITED?

Historical trauma occurs when children of trauma survivors suffer the same trauma symptoms as their parents without ever directly experiencing the trauma themselves. The US Department of Health and Human Services defines historical trauma as "multigenerational trauma experienced by a specific cultural, racial or ethnic group."[7] Major events such as slavery, wars, or genocides are considered historical traumas. Children of trauma survivors may experience higher levels of behavioral, mental, and health issues, including anxiety, aggression, suicide, and heart disease. How trauma is passed from one generation to another is still unclear. "The conundrum with a phenomenon like this is how much of it is biological . . . versus social transmission of information," says Brian Dias, an assistant professor of psychiatry and behavioral sciences at Emory University. "I think there is compelling evidence on both sides of those mechanisms."[8]

experience more stress, depression, and conflict than those in higher-income families. Low-income families have a harder time bouncing back from challenges such as job loss and divorce and fewer options for balancing childcare and work. These challenges can reduce parents' caregiving abilities and limit their resources.

Half of Black and Hispanic children live in low-income households, which means that not all races and ethnicities experience ACEs equally. Sixty-one percent of Black non-Hispanic children and 51 percent of Hispanic children experience one or more ACEs. That's compared to 40 percent of white non-Hispanic children and 23 percent of Asian children.[9]

HEALING FROM ACES AND TRAUMA

No one who experiences ACEs is responsible for the trauma he or she experienced. Likewise, no child who experiences ACEs is irreparably impaired. There are a number of therapeutic approaches and responses that can provide positive outcomes.

Recovery begins with first recognizing that the trauma happened. If desired, teens can take the ACEs quiz online and get their scores. If it is safe to do so, they can talk with someone they trust about what they've experienced. Teens who have experienced ACEs fare better when they ask for and receive help.

Teens also thrive when they develop strong, responsive relationships with at least one caring adult, such as a teacher, family member, or mental health professional. They can also connect with a caring community, whether through a trauma support group, friends, or a religious group. Research shows that strong social ties

> "IT IS IMPORTANT TO REMEMBER THAT YOU ARE NOT POWERLESS. IN FACT, YOU HAVE CONTROL OVER MANY THINGS—INCLUDING HOW CONVERSATIONS PLAY OUT."[10]
>
> —ILANA, 22

While some therapy sessions may cause people to feel strong emotions, attending therapy helps people work through trauma and ACEs.

improve the brain's ability to recover from trauma. Knowing that they are not alone helps teens heal.

While traumatized teens may struggle from the effects of trauma, they can learn important life skills such as self-awareness, focus, and emotional regulation to begin to recover and thrive. These skills can be mastered with practice and time. Learned life skills can prepare teens to better cope with stress and have healthier adult relationships. When teens embrace the process of recognizing, getting help with, and recovering from childhood traumas, they gain the wisdom and resilience needed to move into adulthood.

TEENS IN ABUSIVE ROMANTIC RELATIONSHIPS

Teens can become involved with abusive romantic partners. Their partner may hit, threaten, stalk, verbally abuse, or try to control them. Nearly 1.5 million high school students report suffering abuse from their partners each year.[11] Teens in abusive relationships may try to hide the abuse from friends and caregivers. They may feel as if there is nowhere to turn.

Additionally, friends of a teen in an abusive relationship may not know how to help. One way friends can help is by listening to the person being abused. They should also understand that the person may not feel safe to leave the relationship. Blaming and belittling an abuse victim only makes it harder for her or him to take action. Friends can, however, continue to encourage the person to get help.

Teens in abusive relationships can visit loveisrespect.org, a confidential, anonymous resource provided by the National Domestic Violence Hotline. Teens can also call 1-866-331-9474 or text "loveis" to 22522.

Getting outside and into nature can help relieve stress.

CHAPTER SEVEN

COPING STRATEGIES AND SELF-CARE

Teens dealing with stress, conflict, and sudden changes at home may feel overwhelmed. In response, they can develop ways to feel better, also known as coping strategies. Coping strategies can be excellent ways for teens to take care of themselves. Coping strategies can provide relief from negative emotions.

However, not all coping strategies are equally effective. Some coping strategies cause more problems and allow teens to avoid facing the real conflicts. And some negative coping strategies are addictive or even dangerous.

NEGATIVE COPING STRATEGIES

Negative coping strategies include anything that feels good for a short amount of time but in the end leaves teens worse off than when they started. Examples of negative coping include numbing emotions with food, drugs, alcohol, and sex. These things not only fail to solve the original conflicts but can also have consequences that create additional problems for teens.

Other negative ways to cope with stress include fighting, playing too many video games, undereating or overeating, overexercising, self-harming, and withdrawing from social circles. Teens may also cope with stress and negative emotions by ignoring them. However, ignoring problems does not make them go away and often makes them worse.

Negative coping strategies feel good because they provide temporary relief and a sense of control. However, these coping strategies can also become addictive. The more often teens use these strategies, the more likely they are to become addicted to them and harm themselves by using them. As a result of using negative coping

> "EVERYONE MUST FACE DIFFICULT SITUATIONS, AND EVERYONE MUST COME UP WITH EFFECTIVE WAYS TO DEAL WITH AND BOUNCE BACK FROM THESE SITUATIONS. THIS IS WHY COPING IS A VITAL HUMAN BEHAVIOR, ONE THAT IS NECESSARY FOR SUCCESSFULLY NAVIGATING THROUGH THE CHALLENGING AND OFTEN MURKY OBSTACLE COURSE THAT IS LIFE."[1]
>
> —COURTNEY ACKERMAN, ORGANIZATIONAL PSYCHOLOGY RESEARCHER

Some teens may play video games excessively in order to escape conflict.

strategies, teens also have to deal with their results, which can include substance addictions, unhealthy weight gain or loss, sexually transmitted infections (STIs), complicated romantic relationships, and unplanned pregnancies.

DEVELOPING HEALTHY COPING SKILLS

Many safe and healthy coping skills exist. Healthy coping skills are those that help teens feel better without causing them harm. These skills don't provide quick fixes to problems. Instead, they allow teens to develop the resilience and wisdom to cope with life's difficulties. Healthy coping skills lead teens to positive outcomes and happier, more successful lives.

Self-care is anything that someone can do to improve emotional and physical health. Good self-care begins with taking care of basic needs for good nutrition, exercise, and sleep. Good nutrition involves eating plenty of fruits, vegetables, proteins, and whole grains, while limiting processed foods such as sugary desserts and salty snacks. Good nutrition promotes mood regulation, fends off mental fogginess, and provides teens with much-needed energy.

Exercise reduces the body's stress response and helps teens improve focus. A 2004 study showed that just 15 to 30 minutes of daily exercise can

SOMATIC THERAPY

Somatic psychotherapists use the relationship between body and mind to help their patients. They theorize that trauma impacts the autonomic nervous system, which is responsible for unconscious bodily functions, such as breathing, heart rate, and digestion. This disruption can lead to physical symptoms, such as high blood pressure, anxiety, and digestive issues.

Somatic techniques help patients recover by reducing the physical discomfort resulting from trauma. Somatic treatments include talk therapy as well as meditation, breathing exercises, yoga, dance, and massage. Experts believe moving the body with intention may not only improve physical health but also help the mind heal.

also improve moderate anxiety and depression.[2] Sports and workouts can help teens forget their troubles for a time. This can offer a much-needed mental break that helps them recharge.

Team sports and group exercise, such as yoga classes, prevent teens from becoming too isolated.

> "WHEN WE FORGET ABOUT THE PAST AND LEARN FROM OUR MISTAKES, WE OPEN UP NEW POSSIBILITIES AND OPPORTUNITIES FOR GROWTH."[4]
> —JUSTIN, 16

According to the AAP, teens require between eight and ten hours of sleep each night. "Regularly sleeping fewer than the number of recommended hours is associated with attention, behavior, and learning problems," according to a 2016 statement by the AAP. "Insufficient sleep also increases the risk of accidents, injuries, hypertension, obesity, diabetes, and depression."[3] To form good sleep habits, the National Sleep Foundation recommends that teens establish regular bedtime routines and stick with them on weekends, which helps teens' bodies form natural sleep rhythms. Teens can also avoid caffeine, exercise, and screens during the last few hours before bed to aid sleep.

No good self-care routine would be complete without an emotional component. Stress comes with many unpleasant and sometimes overwhelming emotions, such as anger or fear. In the face of such strong feelings, teens may struggle to make thoughtful choices. A 2014 study found, however, that emotional intelligence (EI) or emotional awareness is a key indicator of health and physical wellness. In other words, developing better EI can help teens manage their emotions in healthier ways that lead to better overall health.

The Yale Center for Emotional Intelligence promotes better EI skills through the acronym RULER, which stands for "Recognizing, Understanding, Labeling, Expressing, and Regulating." Improving EI involves learning to accurately recognize

EMOTIONAL INTELLIGENCE

Emotional intelligence (EI) is the ability to perceive, access, understand, and regulate emotions in order to grow. Researchers link EI with the strength of people's relationships and their academic and professional successes. The five components of EI are self-awareness, self-regulation, motivation, empathy, and social skills. Research shows that these five desirable traits make people better leaders. People with these skills are also more resilient.

Developing EI begins with building better self-awareness. Teens can practice paying attention to their emotions throughout the day. Teens can also get help managing their emotional reactions in ways that are respectful and effective. People with high EI know that moods don't last forever. Teens can shift their moods by choosing to remain positive and motivated even in the face of adversity.

Drinking caffeine can increase feelings of stress and anxiety.

when one is having an emotion, understand the feeling's cause, and label the emotion. Practicing these steps and expressing emotions constructively leads to better emotional regulation.

    Healthy coping skills and self-care routines are unique to each individual. What works for some teens may not work as well for others. Finding the right approach takes time and practice. However, the results will benefit teens well into adulthood with better health, stronger relationships, and more positive outcomes overall.

MEDITATION

Meditation is a popular stress-management tool. It has also been used for centuries in yoga, martial arts, and spiritual traditions. Meditation helps the brain switch out of stress mode and into relaxation mode through physical cues. Research indicates that meditation reduces emotional reactivity, or one's tendency toward knee-jerk reactions when triggered. Studies have also linked meditation with reductions in anxiety, stress, and feelings of loneliness. Meditation improves cognitive function, self-knowledge, and willpower.

Meditators consciously relax their muscles. They focus not on their fears or worries but on taking deep, calming breaths. As a result, they signal their brains to become more calm, focused, and aware. Best of all, meditation can be practiced anywhere by anyone. One simple meditation practice is sitting quietly and breathing slowly to the count of five, repeating for ten minutes.

WHEN TO GET ADDITIONAL HELP

Even with great coping skills and good self-care, teens sometimes need additional support. Needing help is not a sign of weakness. Rather, asking for help is a sign of maturity and self-awareness. When teens ask for help, they are saying that they recognize the importance their communities play in their own development. Getting help also means teens are capable of advocating for their own well-being.

This help could include speaking to a caregiver or other trusted adult such as a teacher or guidance counselor. It may mean speaking to a therapist or addiction counselor. Sometimes, help can start with sharing feelings with a friend.

Some signs that teens need to ask for additional guidance include frequent feelings of exhaustion, worry, hopelessness, or overwhelm. Teens who think about hurting themselves or who lose interest in friends, activities, and eating should also ask for help. Teens who habitually

TEENS OF LGBTQ PARENTS

According to GLAAD, more than ten million people have at least one lesbian, gay, bisexual, transgender, or queer/questioning (LGBTQ) parent.[5] Some teens grow up knowing and readily accepting their parent's orientation and gender identity. Others are surprised and may struggle with complicated feelings when their parents come out.

According to AACAP, research shows children of LGBTQ parents fare as well as children of heterosexual parents. They are also not more likely than children of heterosexual parents to be gay. However, teens of LGBTQ families may face discrimination. They may be bullied or face intrusive or hurtful questions. The AACAP recommends that teens cope with these challenges through open communication with their parents. Teens can talk with their families about how to answer difficult questions and set boundaries. Teens can also build communities of friends with LGBTQ family members for additional support.

use or abuse substances and want to quit may benefit from working with a therapist or an addiction counselor.

    Lastly, if teens have already begun using unhealthy coping strategies, it may take time to replace them with new, healthier strategies. Teens should speak with therapists or other trusted adults who can provide them with resources. Teens can also trust that change will come with continued commitment and practice.

Friends can confide in each other when they are feeling depressed or stressed.

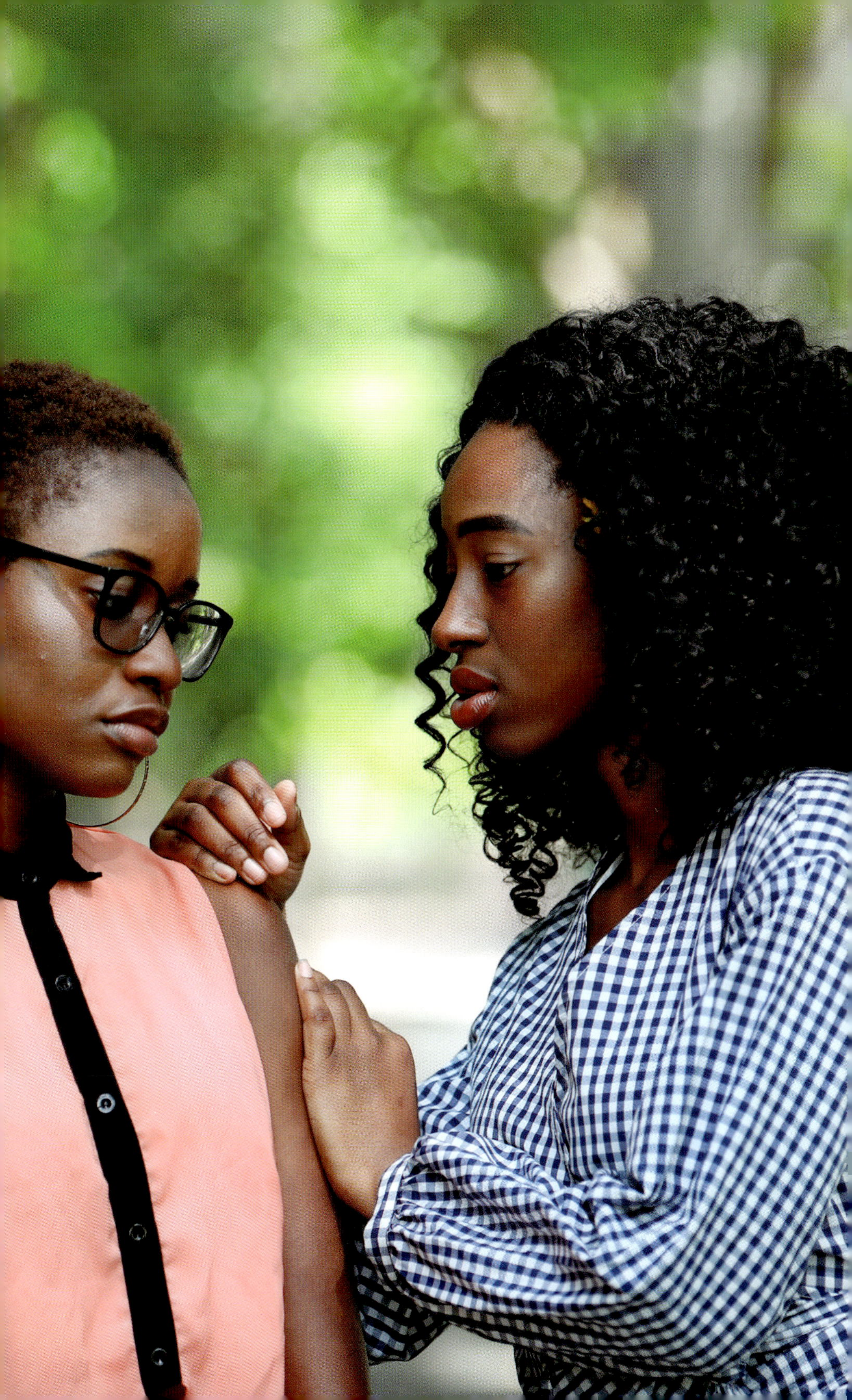

Being prepared for difficult conversations can help people use healthy conflict-resolution strategies instead of unhealthy ones.

CHAPTER EIGHT

HEALTHY CONFLICT RESOLUTION

Disagreements and conflicts can happen between kids and caregivers at any age. However, the teenage years are marked by an increase in such conflicts. Teens are forging their own separate identities, opinions, and tastes. They want to make their own choices, and they want to test the limits set for them.

Caregivers may have a difficult time adjusting to these changes. For many years, caregivers were responsible for their children's every need: what they ate, what time they went to bed, and what clothes they wore. This may no longer be true. However, caregivers are still responsible for their teens' well-being and, in most cases, only want what is best for them.

Teens in blended families may face the unique challenge of accepting their new stepfamilies. They may resent their new family members as intrusions, or they may welcome the new additions to their families. Either way, the pressure to get along with a new caregiver can be intense. The good news is that teens can develop good communication skills to reduce conflict with their caregivers and stepparents.

PREPARING FOR A DIFFICULT CONVERSATION

Good communication between teens and caregivers begins well before conflict arises. Teens can take time throughout the week to talk with caregivers. These simple conversations are time well spent for everyone. Small talk at dinner or during car rides establishes a solid connection between teens and their families. Studies show that teens who feel they can openly talk with their families tend to stay healthy, avoid substance abuse, and not behave violently.

> "GIVING YOURSELF A FEW MINUTES (OR MORE IF YOU'D LIKE!) TO STEADY YOUR BREATH, CALM YOUR THOUGHTS AND GROUND YOURSELF WILL HELP WITH MAINTAINING POSITIVITY."[1]
> —SABREEN, 17

Teens whose families talk openly will be better prepared to discuss conflicts when they arise. Emotions may run high when issues are important to teens. Teens should wait to begin the conversation when they are calm and when caregivers are free and available to talk. Caregivers respond best when teens remain respectful and open to listening. They may not want to begin the conversation in crowded locations or when other family members are present.

The Center for Parent and Teen Communication recommends that teens think through what they want to say ahead of time. They may write down their thoughts so they do not forget. Teens may even want to brainstorm solutions ahead of time and think through possible compromises. Teens should know what they

BOTH SIDES OF THE STORY

It is possible for two family members to experience the same events and see them differently. While both views are limited and flawed on their own, each person's perspective also provides meaning and context to the other's experience. In every conflict, each person's view is true for them. It can be difficult to understand where another person is coming from, though. No one can read another person's mind or intentions.

Experts recommend that family members consider there can be more than one way to see any situation. Family members can also look for problematic patterns of relating that limit progress, such as lying, name-calling, or belittling, and work together to change them. By engaging in healthy conflict, families can reach complete resolution by developing compromises on issues and finding ways to meet everyone's needs.

CONFLICT STYLES

Families can have different conflict styles. Some families avoid conflict in favor of harmony. Others see arguments as ways to resolve differences.

Conflict avoiders value harmony and relationship above directness. They're uncomfortable with strong, negative emotions and outbursts. Conflict avoiders may back away physically during arguments. They may agree too quickly to end the conversation. While avoiding conflict may relieve stress in the short term, families who often avoid conflict don't have the opportunity to work through their differences.

Conflict seekers, on the other hand, use conflict as a way to be seen and heard. They value directness and honesty. Conflict seekers raise their voices and lean in toward the other person when they speak. They may try to dominate others. Conflict seekers want others to see that they are right. Resolving conflict is rarely a straightforward process. Conflicts can take many attempts to be resolved. Understanding the role personality types play in conflict resolution is a helpful way to begin.

hope to accomplish but also set realistic expectations. Everything may not turn out the way they hope.

GOOD COMMUNICATION

"Important conversations can be difficult," says Sarah Hinstorff of the Center for Parent and Teen Communication. "That difficulty often reflects their importance. It's hard to bring up topics like getting in trouble at school, asking for more independence, or talking about relationships, but it's important to talk about these kinds of issues with your parents."[2]

During these conversations, teens should listen and consider their caregivers' viewpoints. Listening with respect means hearing what the other person says. It also means considering others' feelings and motives without dismissing them. Caregivers were teens once too, and they may have valuable perspectives to share. Being a thoughtful listener during a conversation also encourages others to do the same. Teens who want to be heard can start with listening well.

Following a few guidelines will keep the discussion productive and increase the chances of a satisfying resolution. First, teens should try not to take

JOURNALING

Resolving conflict begins with teens knowing how they feel and what they want. But how do teens figure all that out? One possibility is by keeping a journal. Journaling is the practice of writing down one's thoughts in a notebook or diary. Studies show that teens who journal benefit both physically and emotionally. Expressive writing helps teens release tension, which strengthens immunity and lowers blood pressure. Writing down thoughts and feelings can also help teens better express their emotions and pinpoint their triggers.

Journaling increases self-awareness and well-being, just as when talking to a close friend. A journal also offers teens a safe place to question and explore their own likes, dislikes, opinions, fears, and dreams. Journaling helps teens find answers to their most burning questions, and it also provides them with a creative outlet and a positive tool for self-care.

Families who practice good communication, such as by using "I" statements, often develop lasting, positive ways to resolve conflicts.

things personally. This can be easier said than done, but separating caregivers from the idea or concept that is being debated can help.

Teens can use "I" statements to communicate how they feel. For example, "I feel disrespected when you do not knock before entering my room." Teens should focus on communicating their own perspectives while also considering caregivers' perspectives. Putting down others' ideas, using sarcasm, or making derogatory comments will shut down the conversation instead of opening it.

To resolve the conflict, teens can avoid getting off track by staying focused on a single issue. Bringing up the past almost always backfires. People tend to feel defensive. The conversation often grinds to a halt.

WHEN GOOD COMMUNICATION IS NOT ENOUGH

In some cases, teens may be unable to resolve differences

RULES OF FIGHTING FAIR

How families fight is as important as why. According to the University of Texas at Austin Counseling and Mental Health Center, following some basic ground rules of fair fighting can lead to better outcomes. First, family members should argue when they are calm. Staying calm ensures that they will not say or do something they do not intend and will later regret. Family members should agree to take breaks and not act out physically if their emotions get the best of them. Second, family members should be clear about what they want to accomplish and why it is important to them. The goal of the argument should be to find an outcome that is mutually satisfying, not to prove a point. This will require family members to consider one another's needs and views. Finally, family members should agree not to resort to unskillful conflict-resolution approaches. Unskillful approaches include bullying, yelling, intimidation, name-calling, belittling, and making unfair accusations.

Trusted adults can include parents or caregivers, teachers, counselors or therapists, and religious leaders.

with their caregivers. Caregivers may not be reliable or available. Caregivers may not use good communication skills themselves, or they may become abusive or refuse to listen. In other cases, even with the best communication from teens, caregivers will not engage with the problem.

If caregivers are unable to be there for a teen, it may be time for the teen to seek out another trusted adult. Sometimes teens just need to be heard. They need someone to listen. A counselor, therapist, or other family member may be able to help.

Hearing "no" from caregivers can be difficult. However, teens can take time to consider caregivers' refusals. They may find other solutions that are more suitable. Teens can ask for a follow-up discussion but should also respect that caregivers may not be willing to have the same conversation again. Sometimes all that is left is to agree to disagree.

> "YOU'VE GOT TO MEET PEOPLE WHERE THEY ARE AND LOVE THEM AT THE LEVEL THAT THEY CAN RECEIVE IT."[3]
>
> —OPRAH WINFREY, PRODUCER

Knowing when conflict might arise, such as when shopping with family members, can help teens mentally prepare.

CHAPTER NINE

LOOKING AHEAD

Teens can experience changes and conflicts in their families, such as the death of a loved one, abuse and addiction, and family hardship. However, most conflicts between teens and their families are less intense. Conflict can arise between teens and caregivers over something as benign as what they are wearing or how much time they spend on electronic devices. Teens may argue with siblings over television remotes or access to the family car.

DAILY FAMILY CONFLICTS

Minor negative interactions can become so frequent that they are normalized and nearly invisible. However, when they remain unaddressed, these daily conflicts can wear down family relationships. They can also negatively affect teens, including how they perform in school and

> "CONFLICT, EVEN WHEN HANDLED WELL, TAKES TIME AND TREMENDOUS MENTAL ENERGY."[1]
> —LISA DAMOUR, PSYCHOLOGIST

GOAL SETTING FOR TEENS

Teens may find it helpful to set reasonable goals for themselves during times of conflict and change. The first step is to decide on an overall goal, such as, "I want to improve my relationship with my parents." Then, choose steps to take that are specific and measurable, such as, "I want to improve my relationship with my parents by eating dinner with them every weeknight for six weeks." By posting this goal in a visible place, such as the bathroom mirror or a laptop screen, and sharing the goal with friends or family members, teens can hold themselves accountable to completing their goals. Over time, it may feel frustrating to stick to goals, especially if obstacles or challenges arise. But persevering through these obstacles can be made easier by asking others for encouragement.

in extracurricular activities.

According to a 2015 study sponsored by the National Institutes of Health, teens who argued with caregivers were more likely to do poorly at school. The opposite was true as well. When teens struggled at school, they were more likely to have conflicts at home with caregivers. This type of effect is known as spillover.

Many experts believe spillover happens because something that affects one family member often affects every other person in the family. Developing adolescents are especially vulnerable to the impact of high family conflict, particularly when it is with their caregivers. The 2015 study found that experiencing high levels of conflict with caregivers was associated with mental health symptoms and reduced well-being in teens.

Many times, conflicts and changes are not within teens' control. This can lead to feelings of helplessness for teens. Teens may also feel overwhelmed. Researchers recommend that teens and caregivers reduce conflict by understanding and accepting the stages of adolescent development. By understanding that conflict and disagreement are normal parts of growing into an adult, both teens and caregivers can alleviate some sources of family stress.

Caregivers can give teens appropriate

GET RID OF STRESS OUTDOORS

Reducing stress can be as easy as getting outside. Researchers looked at 140 studies of 290 million people in 20 different countries. They reported a link between spending at least two hours per week in green spaces and good physical and mental health.[2] Green spaces include forests, local parks, gardens, and urban environments with vegetation. The two hours could be all at once or over a period of days. The research found that benefits included reduced blood pressure, heart rate, and stress. Teens who live in urban settings can also benefit from nature, says Danielle Shanahan, a research fellow at the University of Queensland in Australia. "There is plenty of evidence that you will get a range of benefits even if all you can manage is putting a plant in your room or looking at trees through your window at home."[3]

Teens can express autonomy and individuality through changing their personal styles, such as by choosing their own clothes and dyeing their hair.

autonomy, or the ability to make some choices on their own. These might include choosing which electives to take in school or what time to go to sleep. Responsible teens recognize that with choices come consequences and responsibilities, and they are prepared to accept them.

MAKING LASTING CHANGES

Teens can also do their parts to ensure positive relationships with their caregivers. Adolescents who report a good relationship with at least one caregiver are more likely to also report good physical, mental, and emotional health. Teens can ask parents for help with balancing academics, extracurricular activities, work, and friends with quality family time.

Teens can learn to identify their needs and communicate with their caregivers in constructive and respectful ways. One way teens can improve communication

TEENS COMING OUT TO PARENTS

For many teens, coming out to their parents is a game changer, says the Strong Family Alliance, an organization that supports LGBTQ teens and their families: "As the person coming out, you've been thinking about your LGBTQ identity for years, but it can take time for parents to adjust."[4] The organization recommends that teens think through what they plan to say in advance. They may want to write out a script and use it during the conversation. Coming out takes courage. However, being real and open with parents can be the first step toward stronger family relationships. For more tips and support, teens can visit strongfamilyalliance.org.

> "ALWAYS BE WILLING TO LISTEN IF YOU EXPECT [YOUR CAREGIVERS] TO . . . LISTEN TO YOU. HEALTHY AND PRODUCTIVE CONVERSATIONS NEED TO GO BOTH WAYS."[5]
>
> —GABY, 19

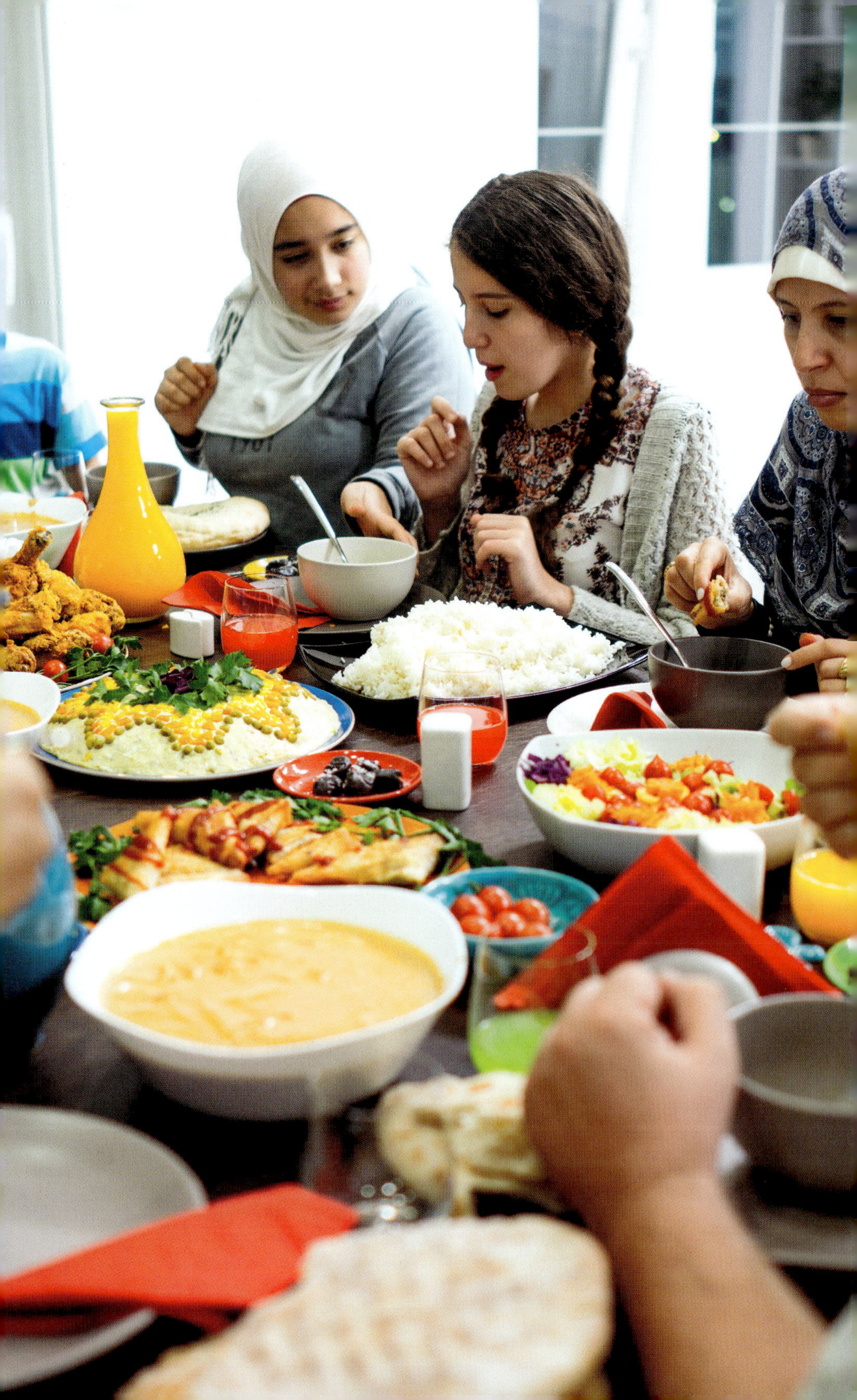

with their caregivers and spend quality time with their families is by eating meals together. Studies show that when teens eat meals with their families they tend to get better nutrition and are less likely to abuse substances. Teens may want to make changes about how they relate to their families. They may want to improve their communication skills or learn to set better boundaries. Teens may recognize some unhealthy patterns in how they cope with stress. They may want to find more skillful ways of coping or create supportive self-care routines.

    Adolescence is a time of great challenges and great changes. Making lasting change takes time, practice, and patience. Change also takes asking for help from caregivers, other trusted adults, or family therapists. However, any move toward improving teens' family relationships, emotional intelligence, and overall health will provide teens with benefits that last a lifetime.

Eating meals as a family allows for many opportunities to build resilience and emotional intelligence.

ESSENTIAL FACTS

FACTS ABOUT FAMILY CONFLICTS AND CHANGES

- A family is made up of one or more caregivers and a child or children.

- The phrase *family of origin* refers to the significant caretakers and siblings a person grows up with. Early experiences within a family of origin strongly influence how a person operates in the world.

- Negative and traumatic childhood experiences and stressful conflicts can compromise later adult health and relationships. Alternatively, a person who receives conflict-management tools will take those skills into the adult world.

IMPACT ON DAILY LIFE

- While every family is different, all families experience some type of change. Change often leads to conflict.

- Families may disagree, debate, or fight to have their needs or desires met. Changes that are large, sudden, unexpected, or irreversible lead to the most intense conflicts. How families cope with conflict depends on family dynamics, such as social structure, relational style, and family history.

- Additional sociological factors such as race, economic status, culture, and religion affect the conflicts families face.
- While conflict is inevitable in relationships, prolonged, unresolved conflict creates chronic stress. Chronic stress is linked with negative health consequences for teens, as well as poor academic performance.

DEALING WITH FAMILY CONFLICTS AND CHANGES

- When handled unskillfully, conflict can damage family members' relationships. When handled in a healthy way, conflict strengthens relationships and builds trust.
- The goal of conflict should always be resolution. Through conflict resolution, teens develop maturity, emotional intelligence, and self-awareness—skills that will carry over into adulthood and improve future relationships and outcomes too.

QUOTE

"In advocating for ourselves, we need to make space for other people to question or disagree."

—Gaby, 19

GLOSSARY

adolescence
The period between childhood and adulthood when a young person grows up, beginning at the onset of puberty.

consent
The process of obtaining explicit and clear permission to cross someone's physical boundaries. Consent must be given without pressure, guilt, or manipulation; refers only to the specific activity for which it's obtained; and can be taken back at any time.

depression
A common but serious mental illness characterized by lasting sadness and anxious feelings that interfere with normal daily activities.

disparity
A great difference.

egalitarian
Having the principle that all people are equal.

family systems theory
A theory in psychiatry that looks at a person's family as a whole in order to understand the individual.

immigrant
A person who permanently moves to a new country.

incarcerated
Held against one's will for committing a crime or while awaiting trial.

racism
Inferior treatment of a person or group of people based on race.

toxic
Very bad, unpleasant, or harmful; poisonous.

trigger
An event or situation that causes someone to do something or feel a certain way.

ADDITIONAL RESOURCES

SELECTED BIBLIOGRAPHY

Brackett, Marc. *Permission to Feel: Unlocking the Power of Emotions to Help Our Kids, Ourselves, and Our Society Thrive*. Macmillan Publishers, 2019.

Gallo, Amy. "Dealing with Conflict Avoiders and Seekers." *Harvard Business Review*, 6 Apr. 2017, hbr.org. Accessed 31 May 2020.

Jensen, Frances E., and Amy Ellis Nutt. *The Teenage Brain: A Neuroscientist's Survival Guide to Raising Adolescents and Young Adults*. HarperCollins, 2015.

FURTHER READINGS

Kissen, Debra, et al. *Rewire Your Anxious Brain for Teens: Using CBT, Neuroscience, and Mindfulness to Help You End Anxiety, Panic, and Worry*. New Harbinger Publications, 2020.

Lusted, Marcia Amidon. *Puberty*. Abdo, 2022.

Myers, Carrie. *Coping with Stress and Pressure*. Abdo, 2021.

ONLINE RESOURCES

Booklinks NONFICTION NETWORK
FREE! ONLINE NONFICTION RESOURCES

To learn more about family conflicts and changes, please visit **abdobooklinks.com** or scan this QR code. These links are routinely monitored and updated to provide the most current information available.

MORE INFORMATION

For more information on this subject, contact or visit the following organizations:

Center for Parent & Teen Communication

2716 South St., Ninth Floor
Philadelphia, PA 19146
parentandteen.com

The Center for Parent & Teen Communication offers practical, science-based strategies for strengthening family connections and building youth prepared to thrive.

National Center for Child Traumatic Stress

1121 West Chapel Hill St., Ste. 201
Durham, NC 27701
nctsn.org/audiences/youth

The National Center for Child Traumatic Stress at Duke University raises the standard of care and improves access to services for traumatized children, their families, and communities throughout the United States.

National Institute on Drug Abuse for Teens

6001 Executive Blvd., Rm. 5213, MSC 9561
Bethesda, MD 20892
teens.drugabuse.gov/teens

The National Institute on Drug Abuse for Teens provides youth ages 11 to 17 with the facts about drugs and their effects on the brain and body.

SOURCE NOTES

CHAPTER 1. FAMILIES, CONFLICT, AND CHANGE

1. "Parenting in America." *Pew Research Center*, 17 Dec. 2015, pewsocialtrends.org. Accessed 1 Sept. 2020.
2. "Parenting in America."
3. Belinda Luscombe. "The Divorce Rate Is Dropping. That May Not Actually Be Good News." *Time*, 26 Nov. 2018, time.com. Accessed 1 Sept. 2020.
4. Adrian Lam. "How Our Families Influence Our Ideas about Sex." *Sex, Etc.*, 3 Nov. 2016, sexetc.org. Accessed 1 Sept. 2020.
5. Elyssa Barbash. "Realistic Expectations in the Process of Growth and Change." *Psychology Today*, 16 June 2018, psychologytoday.com. Accessed 1 Sept. 2020.

CHAPTER 2. COMMON FAMILY CHANGES

1. Belinda Luscombe. "The Divorce Rate Is Dropping. That May Not Actually Be Good News." *Time*, 26 Nov. 2018, time.com. Accessed 1 Sept. 2020.
2. "Stepfamily Statistics." *Step Family Foundation*, n.d., stepfamily.org. Accessed 1 Sept. 2020.
3. Erin Duffin. "Average Number of Own Children Per US Family with Own Children 1960–2019." *Statista*, 13 Jan. 2020, statista.com. Accessed 1 Sept. 2020.
4. "How Do Families Cope with Financial Shocks?" *Pew Charitable Trusts*, Oct. 2015, pewtrusts.org. Accessed 1 Sept. 2020.
5. Jonathan Strum. "Grief by the Numbers: Facts and Statistics." *Recovery Village*, 8 Apr. 2020, therecoveryvillage.com. Accessed 1 Sept. 2020.
6. Jessica Dickler. "Why So Few Teenagers Have Jobs Anymore." *CNBC*, 6 Oct. 2019, cnbc.com. Accessed 1 Sept. 2020.
7. Martin R. Huecker and William Smock. "Domestic Violence." *StatPearls*, 26 June 2020, ncbi.nlm.nih.gov. Accessed 1 Sept. 2020.
8. Administration for Children and Families. "Child Abuse, Neglect Data Released." *US Department of Health and Human Services*, 28 Jan. 2019, acf.hhs.gov. Accessed 1 Sept. 2020.
9. Gretchen Livingston and Deja Thomas. "Why Is the Teen Birth Rate Falling?" *Pew Research Center*, 2 Aug. 2019, pewresearch.org. Accessed 1 Sept. 2020.
10. "Parenting as a Teenager." *raisingchildren.net.au*, n.d., raisingchildren.net.au. Accessed 1 Sept. 2020.

11. Sarah Hinstorff. "Fix Conflict with Parents." *Center for Parent and Teen Communication*, 4 Sept. 2018, parentandteen.com. Accessed 1 Sept. 2020.
12. "The Effects of Drug Addiction on Family Members." *Behavioral Health of the Palm Beaches*, n.d., bhpalmbeach.com. Accessed 1 Sept. 2020.

CHAPTER 3. FAMILY DYNAMICS

1. "Ethnic and Racial Minorities and Socioeconomic Status." *American Psychological Association*, July 2017, apa.org. Accessed 1 Sept. 2020.
2. Jeanne Batalova et al. "Frequently Requested Statistics on Immigrants and Immigration in the United States." *Migration Policy Institute*, 14 Feb. 2020, migrationpolicy.org. Accessed 1 Sept. 2020.
3. Neema Syovata. "Neema's Story." *Teens Writing about Immigration*, n.d., pbs.org. Accessed 1 Sept. 2020.
4. Jeffrey S. Passel. "Measuring Illegal Immigration: How Pew Research Center Counts Unauthorized Immigrants in the US." *Pew Research Center*, 12 July 2019, pewresearch.org. Accessed 1 Sept. 2020.
5. Cassaundra Rodriguez. "Seven Things to Know about Mixed-Status Families." *National Center for Institutional Diversity*, 5 June 2018, medium.com. Accessed 1 Sept. 2020.
6. "Parenting in America." *Pew Research Center*, 17 Dec. 2015, pewsocialtrends.org. Accessed 1 Sept. 2020.
7. Sarah Hinstorff. "How to Really Be a Good Listener." *Center for Parent and Teen Communication*, 4 Sept. 2018, parentandteen.com. Accessed 1 Sept. 2020.

CHAPTER 4. ADOLESCENCE AND FAMILY CONFLICT

1. Carl E. Pickhardt. "Parenting Adolescents and How Much to Control." *Psychology Today*, 18 Mar. 2019, psychologytoday.com. Accessed 1 Sept. 2020.
2. Kathleen Smith. "6 Common Triggers of Teen Stress." *PsyCom*, 25 Nov. 2018, psycom.net. Accessed 1 Sept. 2020.
3. "Older Youth Housing, Financial Literacy and Other Supports." *National Conference of State Legislatures*, 23 Apr. 2020, ncsl.org. Accessed 1 Sept. 2020.
4. Sarah Hinstorff. "Champion Yourself: Be an Effective Personal Advocate." *Center for Parent and Teen Communication*, 4 Sept. 2018, parentandteen.com. Accessed 1 Sept. 2020.

SOURCE NOTES CONTINUED

CHAPTER 5. TYPES OF FAMILY CONFLICT

1. Cassandra Fetchik. "Draw the Line: Setting Healthy Relationship Boundaries." *Sex, Etc.*, 28 Mar. 2019, sexetc.org. Accessed 1 Sept. 2020.
2. Kate Stringer. "What's an Emotion Scientist? Inside the New Concept Shaping Social-Emotional Learning." *LA School Report*, 5 Aug. 2019, laschoolreport.com. Accessed 1 Sept. 2020.

CHAPTER 6. CONFLICT AND TRAUMA

1. "About the CDC-Kaiser ACE Study." *Centers for Disease Control and Prevention*, 13 Apr. 2020, cdc.gov. Accessed 1 Sept. 2020.
2. Aldo Civico. "3 Steps to Resolving Conflict within Your Family." *Psychology Today*, 4 June 2015, psychologytoday.com. Accessed 1 Sept. 2020.
3. "Got Your ACE Score?" *ACES Too High*, n.d., acestoohigh.com. Accessed 1 Sept. 2020.
4. "Got Your ACE Score?"
5. "Post-Traumatic Growth." *Manitoba Trauma Information and Education Centre*, n.d., trauma-recovery.ca. Accessed 1 Sept. 2020.
6. "Preventing Adverse Childhood Experiences (ACEs): Leveraging the Best Available Evidence." *Centers for Disease Control and Prevention*, 2019, cdc.gov. Accessed 1 Sept. 2020.
7. Administration for Children and Families. "Trauma." *Department of Health and Human Services*, n.d., acf.hhs.gov. Accessed 1 Sept. 2020.
8. Dana G. Smith. "Scientists Are Discovering How Trauma Can Be Inherited." *Elemental*, 24 Jan. 2020, elemental.medium.com. Accessed 1 Sept. 2020.
9. Vanessa Sacks and David Murphey. "The Prevalence of Adverse Childhood Experiences, Nationally, by State, and by Race or Ethnicity." *Child Trends*, 20 Feb. 2018, childtrends.org. Accessed 1 Sept. 2020.
10. Sarah Hinstorff. "Move Tough Conversations Forward." *Center for Parent and Teen Communication*, 4 Sept. 2018, parentandteen.com. Accessed 1 Sept. 2020.
11. "Teen Dating Violence Statistics 2019." *Domestic Violence Services, Inc.*, 2019, dvs-or.org. Accessed 1 Sept. 2020.

CHAPTER 7. COPING STRATEGIES AND SELF-CARE
1. Courtney E. Ackerman. "Coping: Dealing with Life's Inevitable Disappointments in a Healthy Way." *Positive Psychology*, 9 Jan. 2020, positivepsychology.com. Accessed 1 Sept. 2020.
2. Monika Guszkowska. "Effects of Exercise on Anxiety, Depression, and Mood." *Psychiatria Polska*, vol. 38, no. 4, 2004. 611–620.
3. Melissa Jenco. "AAP Endorses New Recommendations on Sleep Times." *AAP News*, 13 June 2016, aappublications.org. Accessed 1 Sept. 2020.
4. Sarah Hinstorff. "Improve Communication and Resolve Conflict: Focus on the Issue at Hand." *Center for Parent and Teen Communication*, 4 Sept. 2018, parentandteen.com. Accessed 1 Sept. 2020.
5. "Children of LGBT Parents." *GLAAD*, n.d., glaad.org. Accessed 1 Sept. 2020.

CHAPTER 8. HEALTHY CONFLICT RESOLUTION
1. Sabreen Dawud. "Self-Care: More Important than Ever." *Sex, Etc.*, 24 Apr. 2020, sexetc.org. Accessed 1 Sept. 2020.
2. Sarah Hinstorff. "Talk to Parents about Something Important." *Center for Parent and Teen Communication*, 4 Sept. 2018, parentandteen.com. Accessed 1 Sept. 2020.
3. Lynn Okura. "The Emotional Lesson Oprah Had to Learn about Her Mother." *HuffPost*, 17 Sept. 2013, huffpost.com. Accessed 1 Sept. 2020.

CHAPTER 9. LOOKING AHEAD
1. Lisa Damour. "How to Help Tweens and Teens Manage Social Conflict." *New York Times*, 16 Jan. 2019, nytimes.com. Accessed 1 Sept. 2020.
2. Kate Lachowycz. "An Exploration of the Relationship between Greenspaces, Physical Activity, and Health." *University of East Anglia*, Sept. 2013, ueaeprints.uea.ac.uk. Accessed 1 Sept. 2020.
3. Alexandra Sifferlin. "The Healing Power of Nature." *Time*, 14 July 2016, time.com. Accessed 1 Sept. 2020.
4. "Coming Out to Your Parents." *Strong Family Alliance*, n.d., strongfamilyalliance.org. Accessed 1 Sept. 2020.
5. Sarah Hinstorff. "Champion Yourself: Be an Effective Personal Advocate." *Center for Parent and Teen Communication*, 4 Sept. 2018, parentandteen.com. Accessed 1 Sept. 2020.

INDEX

abuse, 15, 22–23, 46, 61, 63, 69, 93
adolescence, stages of, 41–43, 95
Adverse Childhood Experiences (ACEs), 62–69
allopregnanolone (THP), 44–45
American Academy of Child and Adolescent Psychiatry (AACAP), 25, 79
American Academy of Pediatrics (AAP), 32, 56, 75
American Psychological Association (APA), 45, 47
anger, 5, 17, 19, 20, 49, 53, 56–57, 76
arguments, 5, 15, 16, 41, 86, 89, 93, 94

blended families, 8–9, 15–17, 83
boundaries, 16, 25, 50, 53, 79, 99
Bureau of Labor Statistics, US, 32

Center for Parent and Teen Communication, 85, 86
Centers for Disease Control and Prevention (CDC), US, 62, 65
Childhelp National Child Abuse Hotline, 23
chores, 5–6
class, 29, 30
compromises, 13, 34, 53, 56, 85
conflict, types of
    conflict styles, 30, 34–37, 86
    daily conflicts, 31, 93–96
    healthy conflicts, 10, 31, 34, 40, 42, 45, 49, 50, 54–59, 83–91
    unhealthy conflicts, 10, 49–54, 90–91

coping strategies, 7, 22, 23, 29, 45, 62, 69, 71–80, 99
custody, 17
difficult conversations, 84–86
divorce, 5, 9, 11–12, 15–17, 30, 31, 34, 64, 66

eating meals together, 56, 84, 94, 99
economic challenges, 9, 17–19, 21, 29, 30, 32–33, 64
emotional intelligence (EI), 57, 76–77, 99
exercise, 45, 72, 74–75
extracurricular activities, 7, 20, 94, 97

family dynamics, 24, 29–37
family of origin, 9–10, 24–25, 39–40
family systems theory, 30
foster care, 46

gender roles, 31
grief, 20–22

health outcomes, 42, 51, 63, 67, 74, 76, 78
homelessness, 19, 62
homeownership, 30
hormones, 39, 45, 50

immigration, 32–33, 35
impulse control, 41–43, 62
incarceration, 32
independence, 7, 37, 40–41, 86
insomnia, 21, 61

journaling, 87

Kaiser Permanente, 62
LGBTQ caregivers and teens, 79, 97
marriage, 8, 15, 19, 30, 44
meditation, 74, 78
mental health, 35, 66, 74–75, 89, 95, 97
mixed-status families, 35
National Alliance for Grieving Children, 22
National Center for Health Statistics, 23
National Conference of State Legislatures, 46
National Domestic Violence Hotline, 10, 69
National Sleep Foundation, 75
neglect, 22–23, 46, 63
nutrition, 56, 74, 99

patience, 57, 64, 99
Pew Research Center, 9, 35, 36–37
puberty, 39

race, 9, 29, 32, 62, 66
religion, 29, 32, 34, 67
resilience, 13, 46–47, 69, 74, 76
resources, 10, 16, 33, 66
responsibility, 20, 21, 24, 34, 52, 53, 83, 96
romantic relationships, 7, 10, 16–17, 23, 26, 41, 63, 69, 73
RULER, 76–77

school, 19, 20 45, 46, 86, 93–94, 96
setting goals, 36, 36, 94
sexually transmitted infections (STIs), 42, 73
siblings, 9, 11, 16, 20, 22, 25, 29, 41, 93
sleep, 45, 56, 74–75, 96
socioeconomic status (SES), 30, 33–34, 65–67
somatic therapy, 74
space, 16, 50
stepfamilies, *see* blended families.
stress, 5, 7, 8, 10, 12, 25, 35, 40, 41, 43–47, 50–52, 56, 57, 61–62, 66, 69, 71–75, 78, 86, 95, 99
substance abuse, 23, 25–26, 73, 80, 84, 99
suicide, 61, 63–64, 66

teen pregnancy, 23–25, 42, 73
THP, *see* allopregnanolone.
trauma, 8, 10, 23, 61, 63, 64–69, 74
    inherited trauma, 66
    post-traumatic growth (PTG), 64
    post-traumatic stress disorder (PTSD), 61

unemployment, 32
University of Texas at Austin Counseling and Mental Health Center, 89

violence, 10, 22–23, 62, 63, 69, 84

Winfrey, Oprah, 91

Yale Center for Emotional Intelligence, 57, 76

ABOUT THE AUTHOR

CHRISTA C. HOGAN

Christa C. Hogan is an author and former licensed foster parent and mother to three boys, one a teen. She also teaches yoga and meditation and enjoys hiking, traveling, reading, and cooking.

ABOUT THE CONSULTANT

KATHLEEN N. BERGMAN, PhD

Kathleen N. Bergman, PhD, is a developmental psychologist at the University of Notre Dame. Her research focuses on adolescent development and interparental and family conflict from a perspective rooted in developmental psychopathology.